Unbridled Spirit

Unbridled Spirit

A Horse Picture Book

ISBN-13: 978-0-9887017-5-5
michaelpaulhoward.net

Photographs by Cindy Howard & Michael Howard
Layout & Design by Michael Howard

Special thanks to:
Lewis Stables, Jonesboro, AR
If Wishes Were Horses, Beech Grove, AR
Lauren Lane, Jonesboro, AR

Foreword

When Cindy was a small girl, she had her own chocolate Shetland pony named Starbuck. She quickly fell in love with Starbuck, and they became best friends. Sadly, one day her parents decided to sell Starbuck, but Cindy never forgot her love for Starbuck or for horses.

Many years later, as an adult and after an illness, Cindy rekindled that love for horses to help her heal mentally and physically.

This picture book is a way of sharing not only a love for horses because of their beauty, but also for their ability to help us heal. We hope you enjoy this book as much as we enjoyed making it.

Cindy & Michael Howard

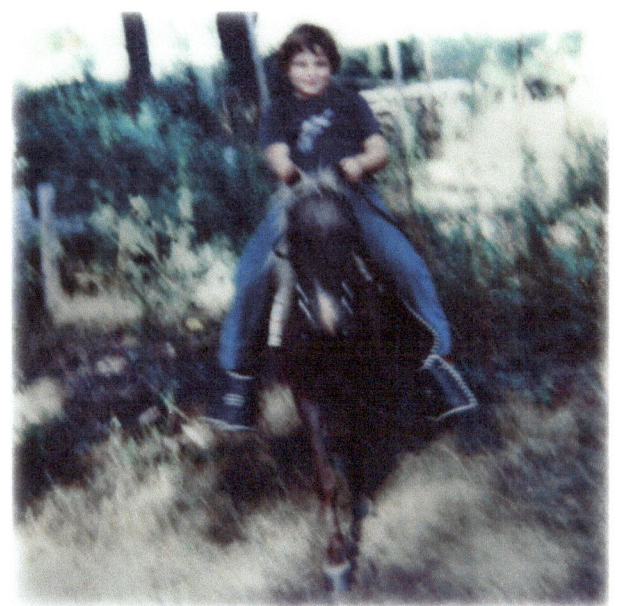

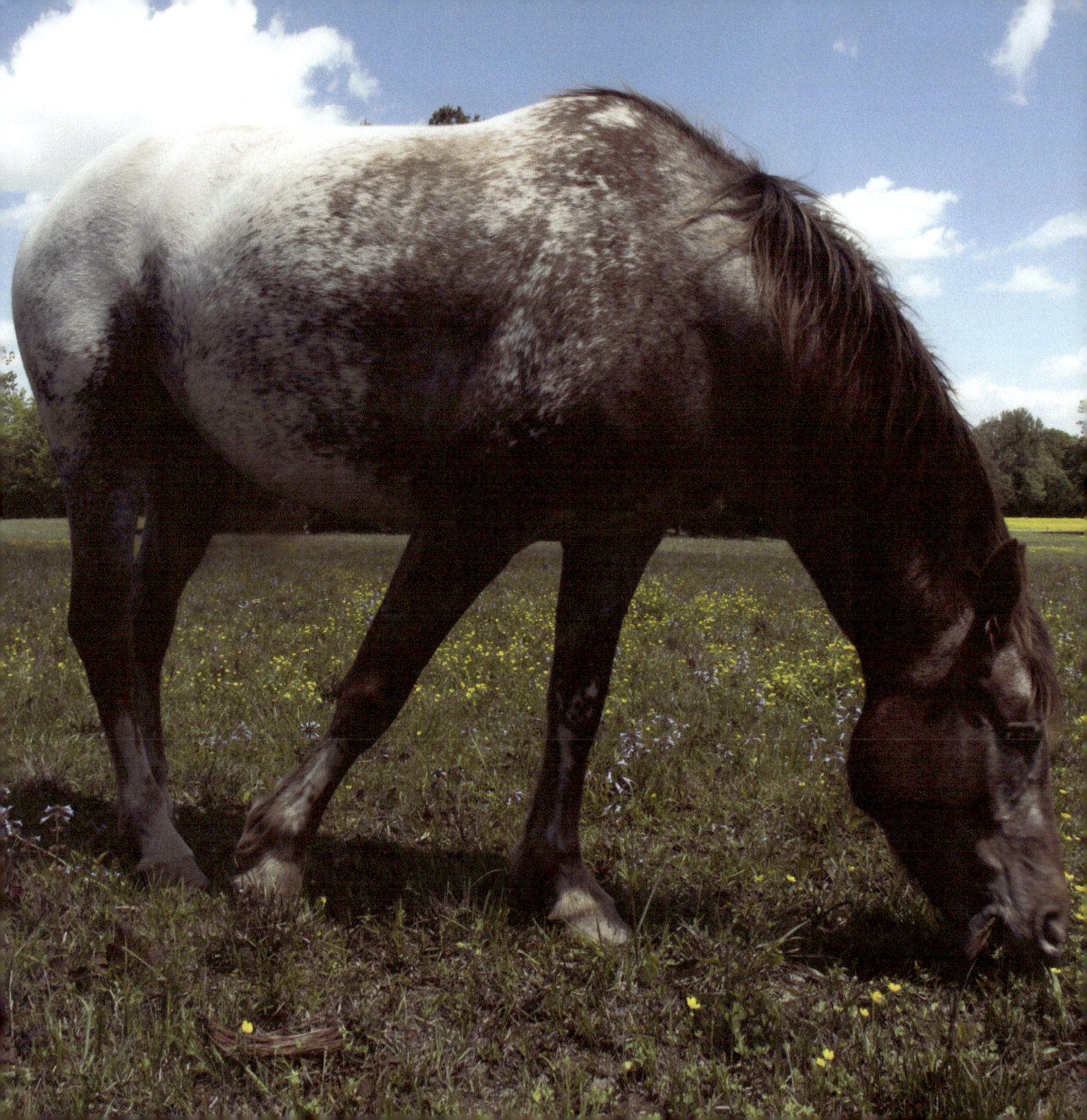

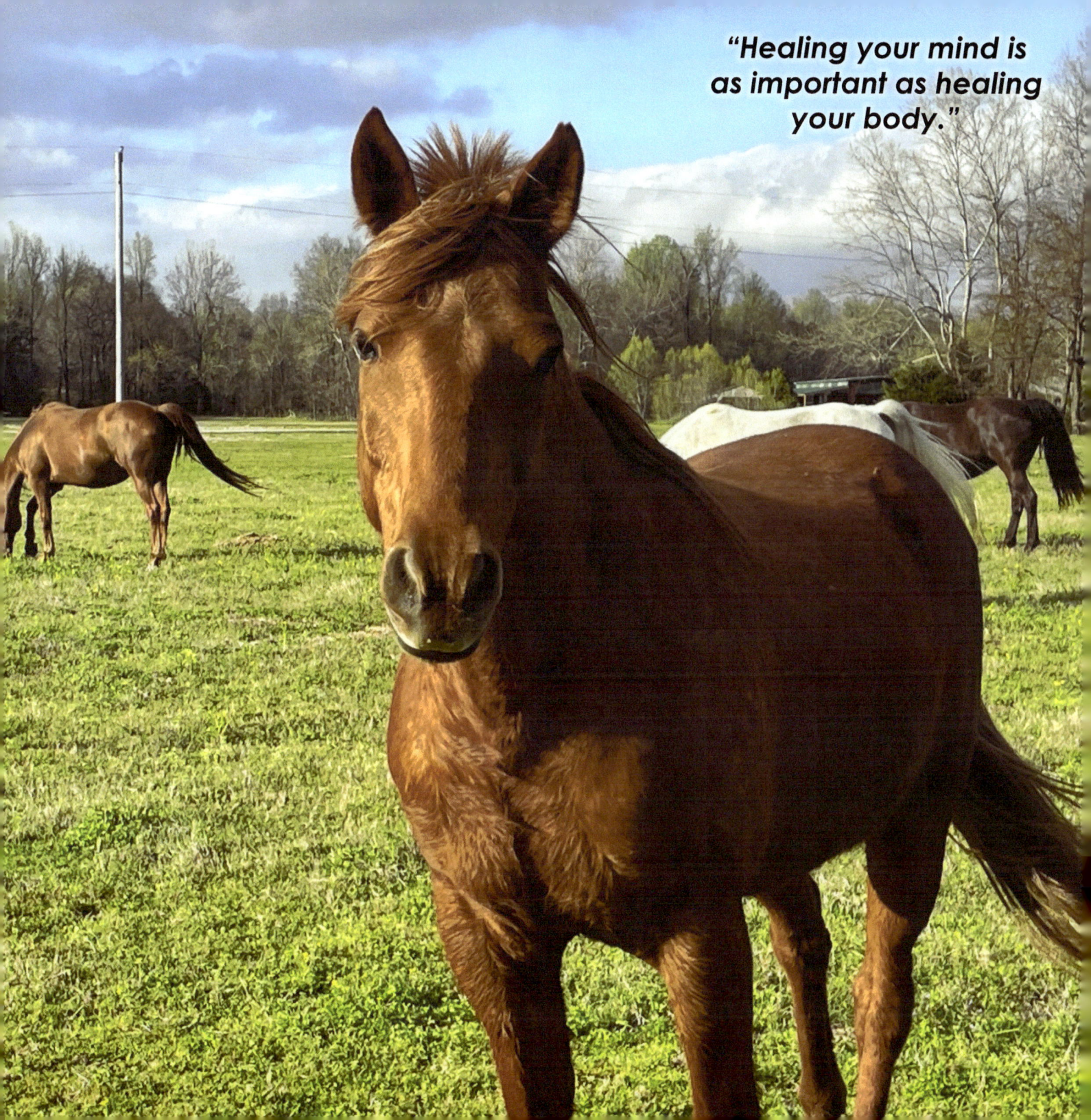

"Healing your mind is as important as healing your body."

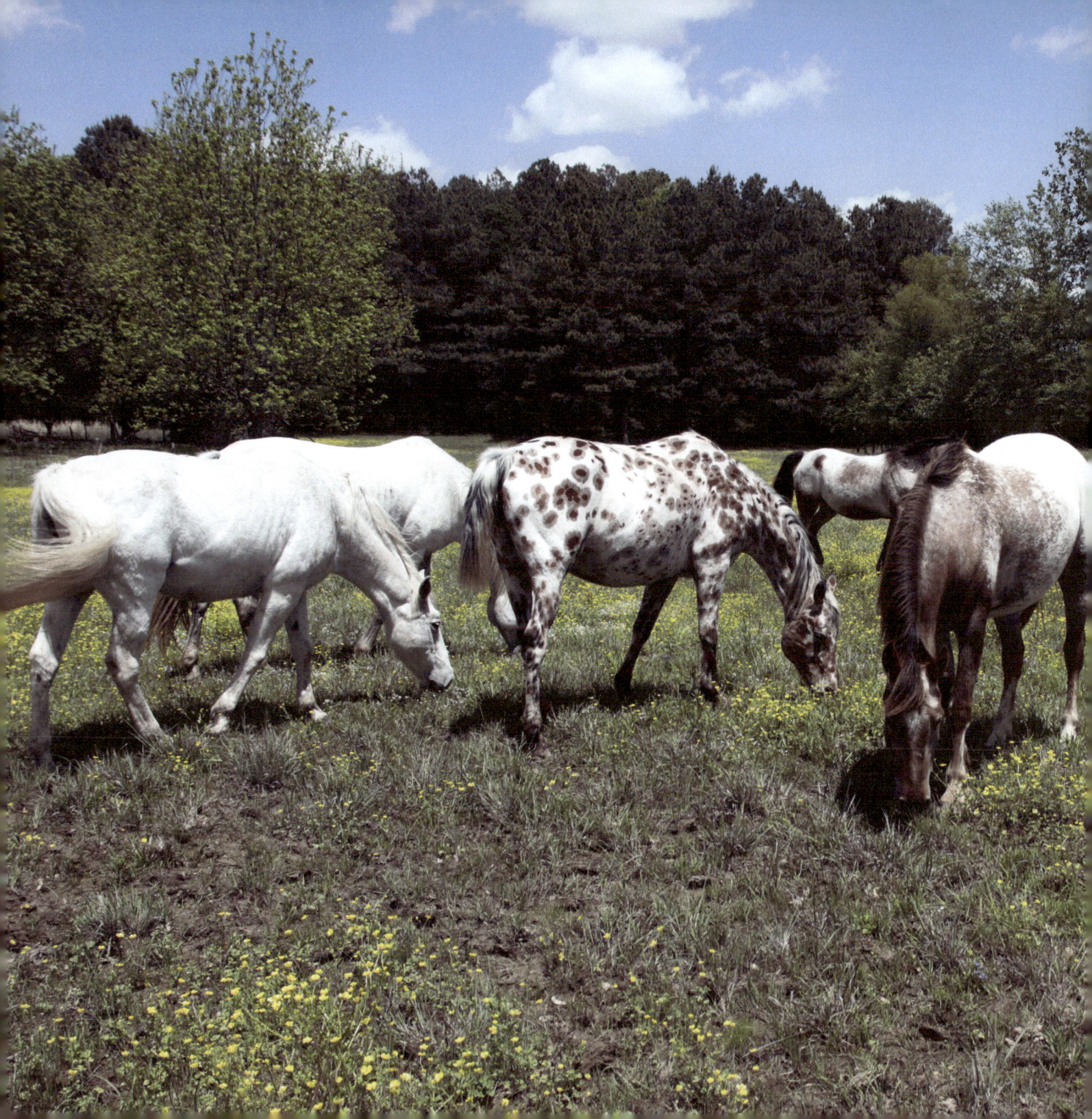

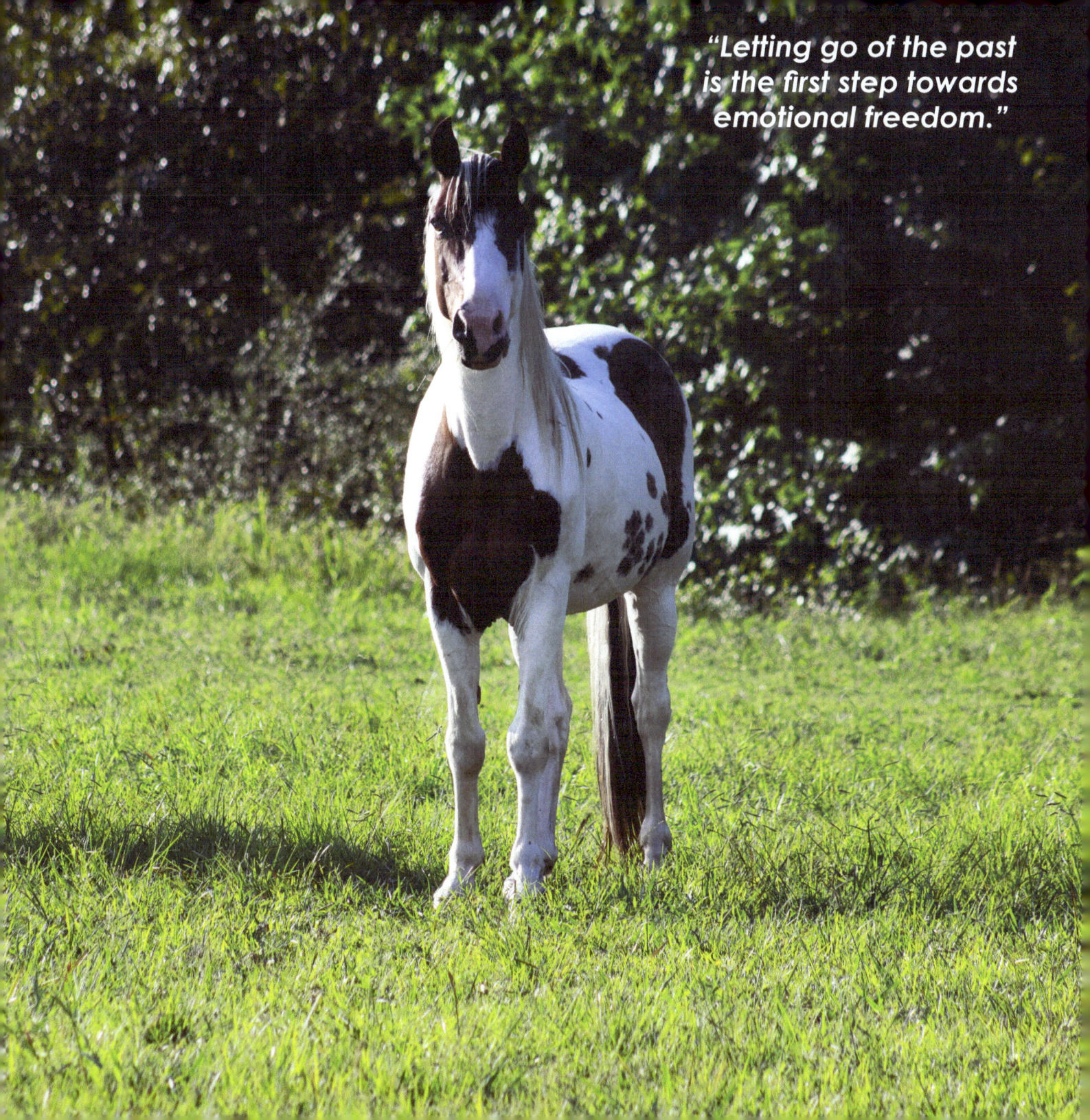

"Letting go of the past is the first step towards emotional freedom."

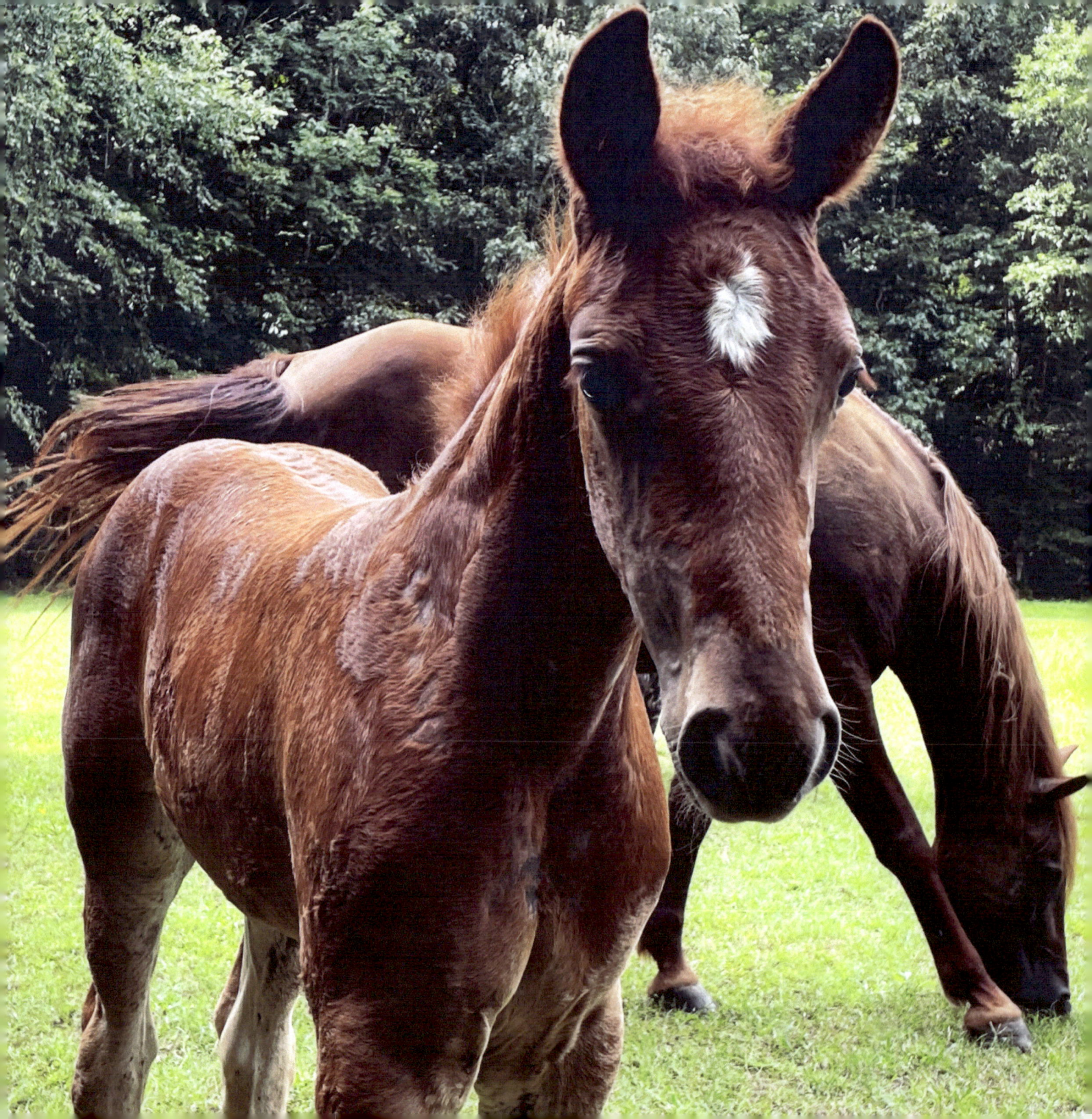

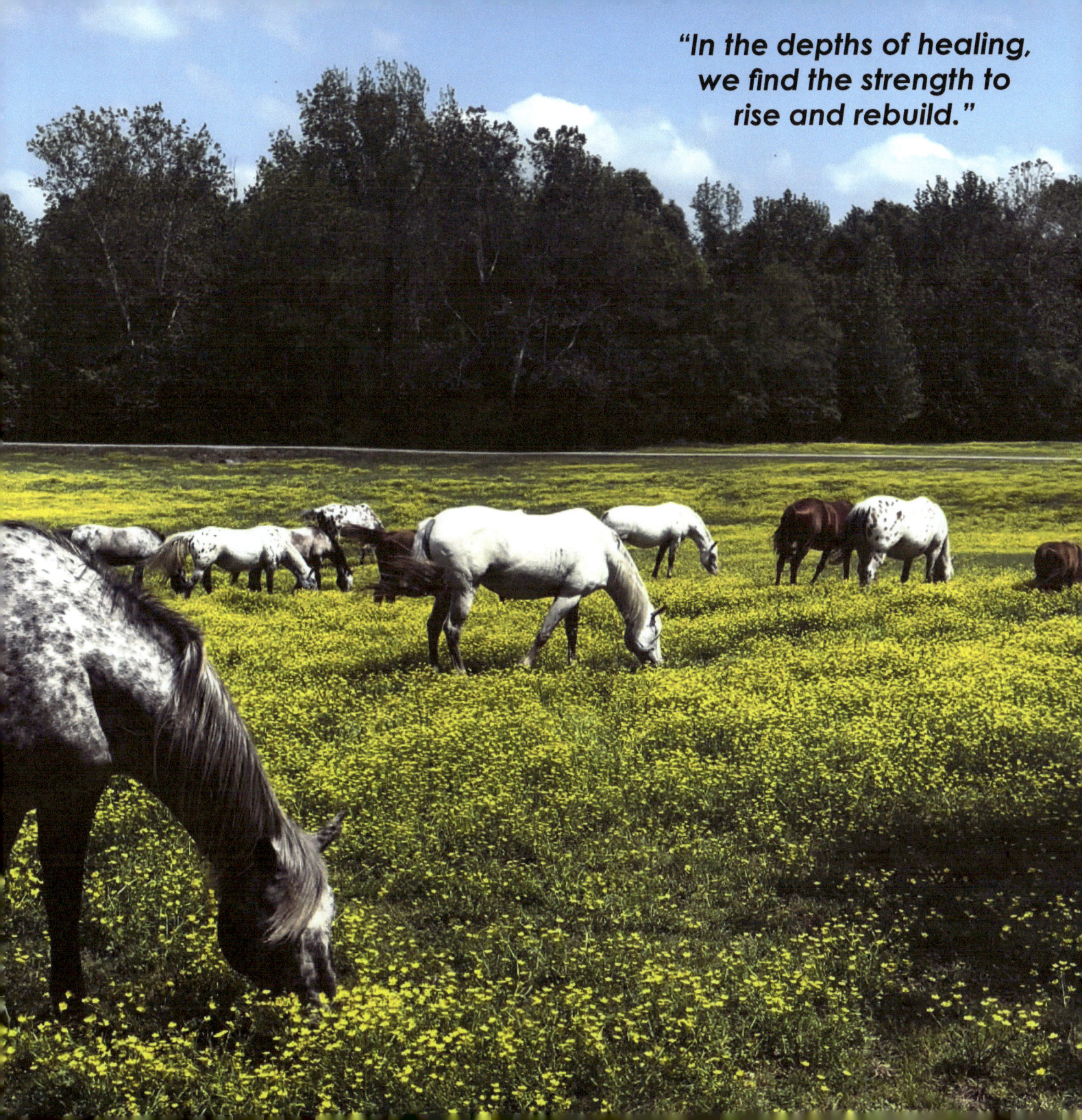

"In the depths of healing,
we find the strength to
rise and rebuild."

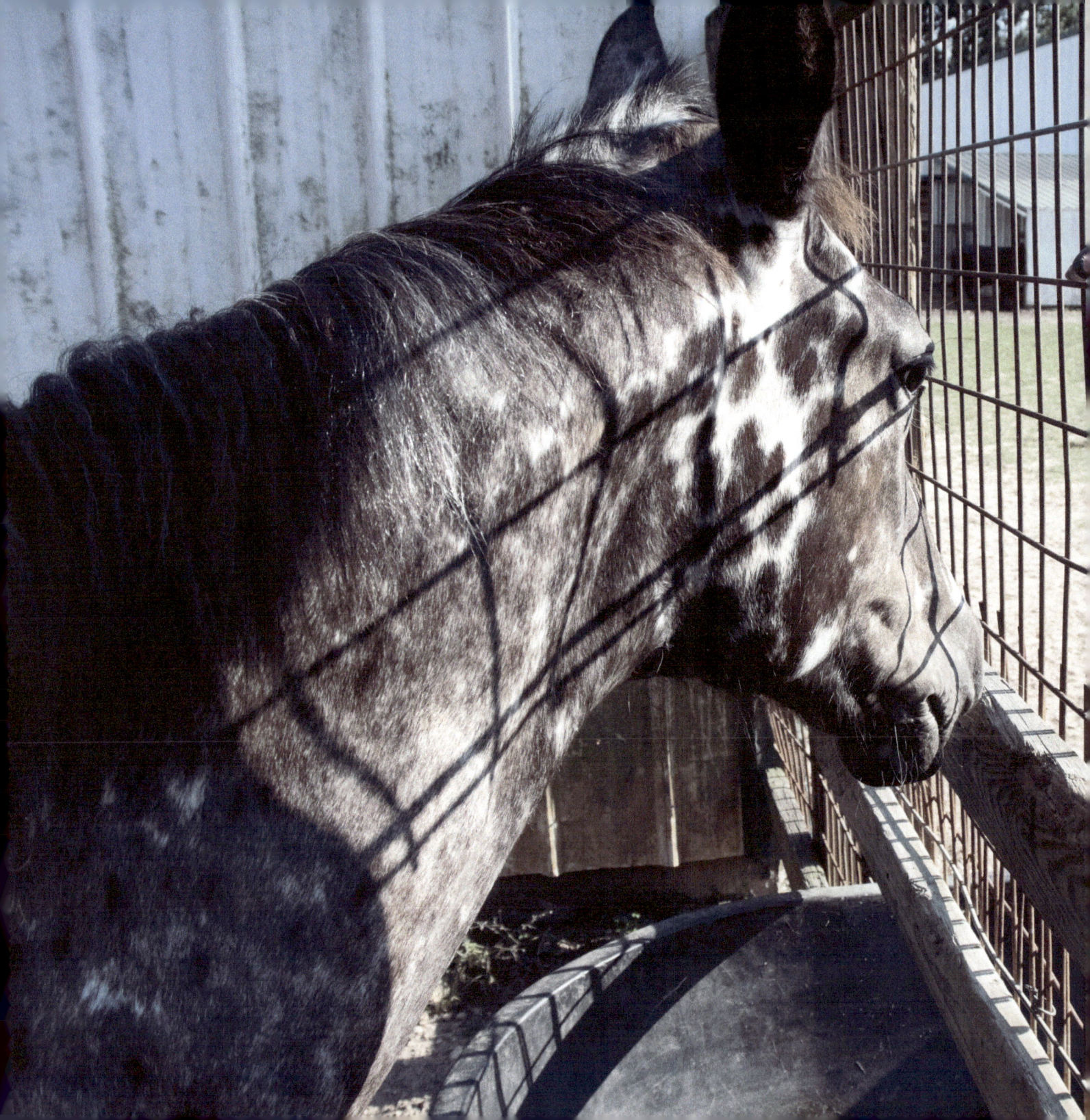

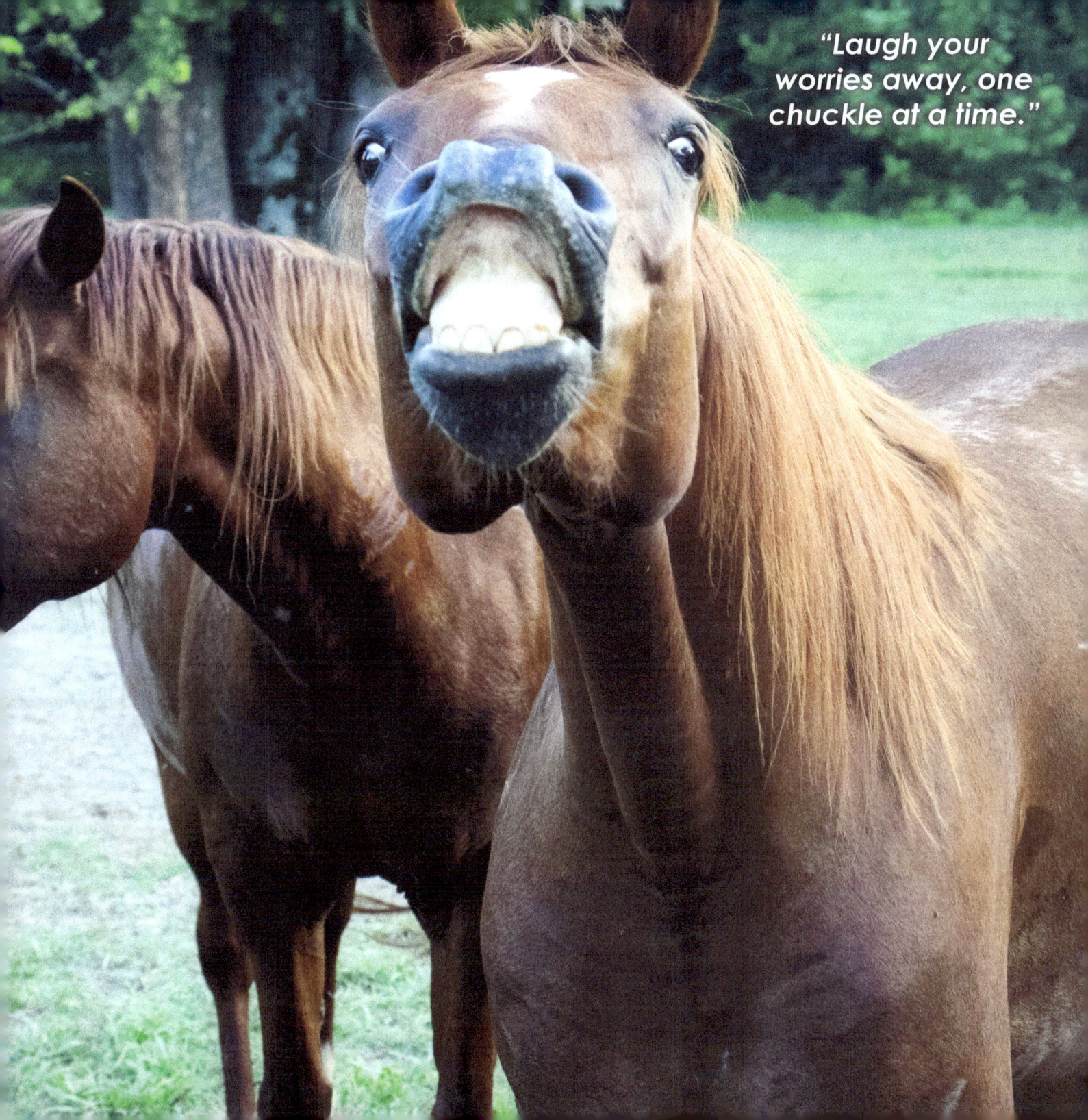

"Laugh your worries away, one chuckle at a time."

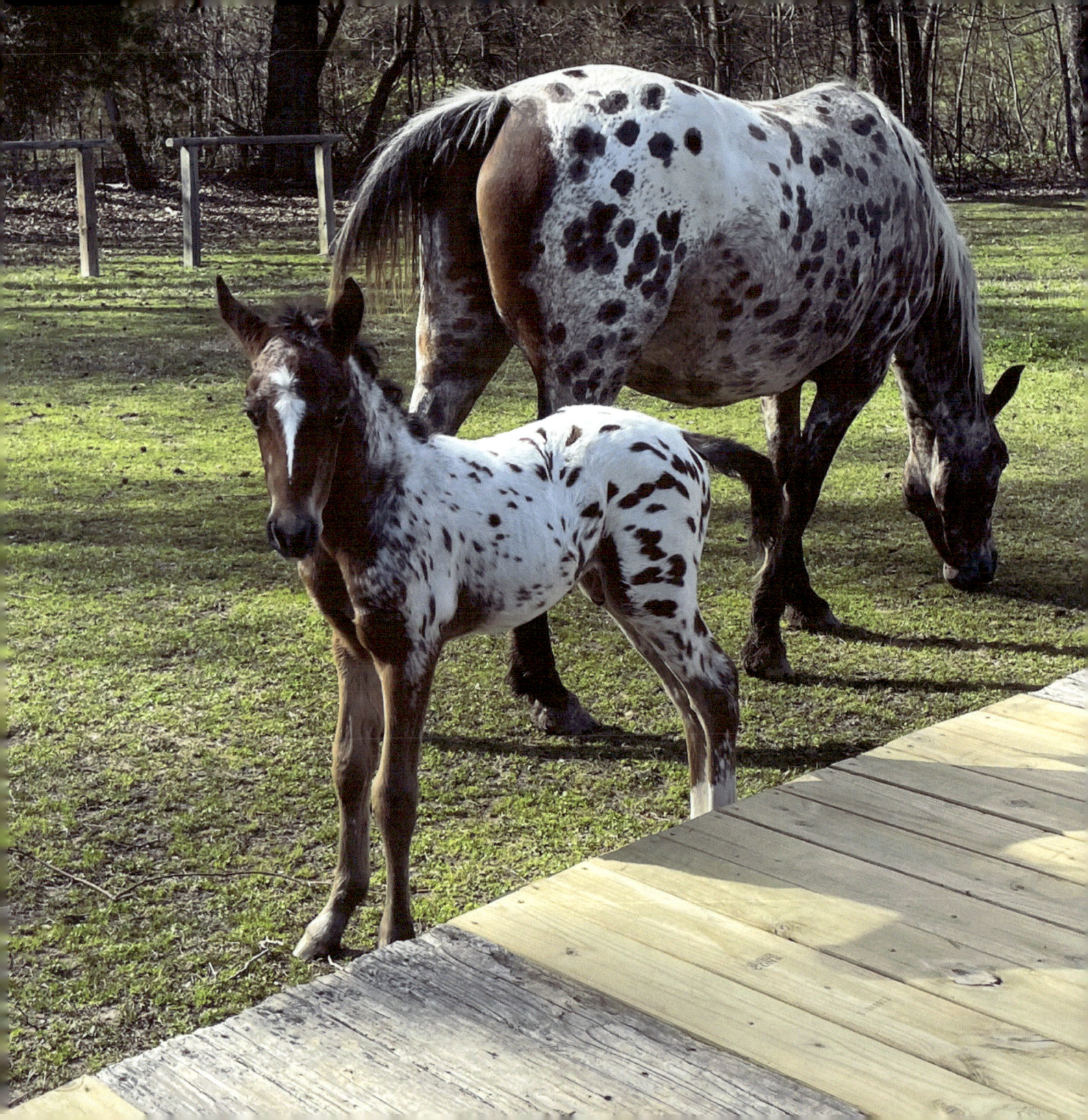

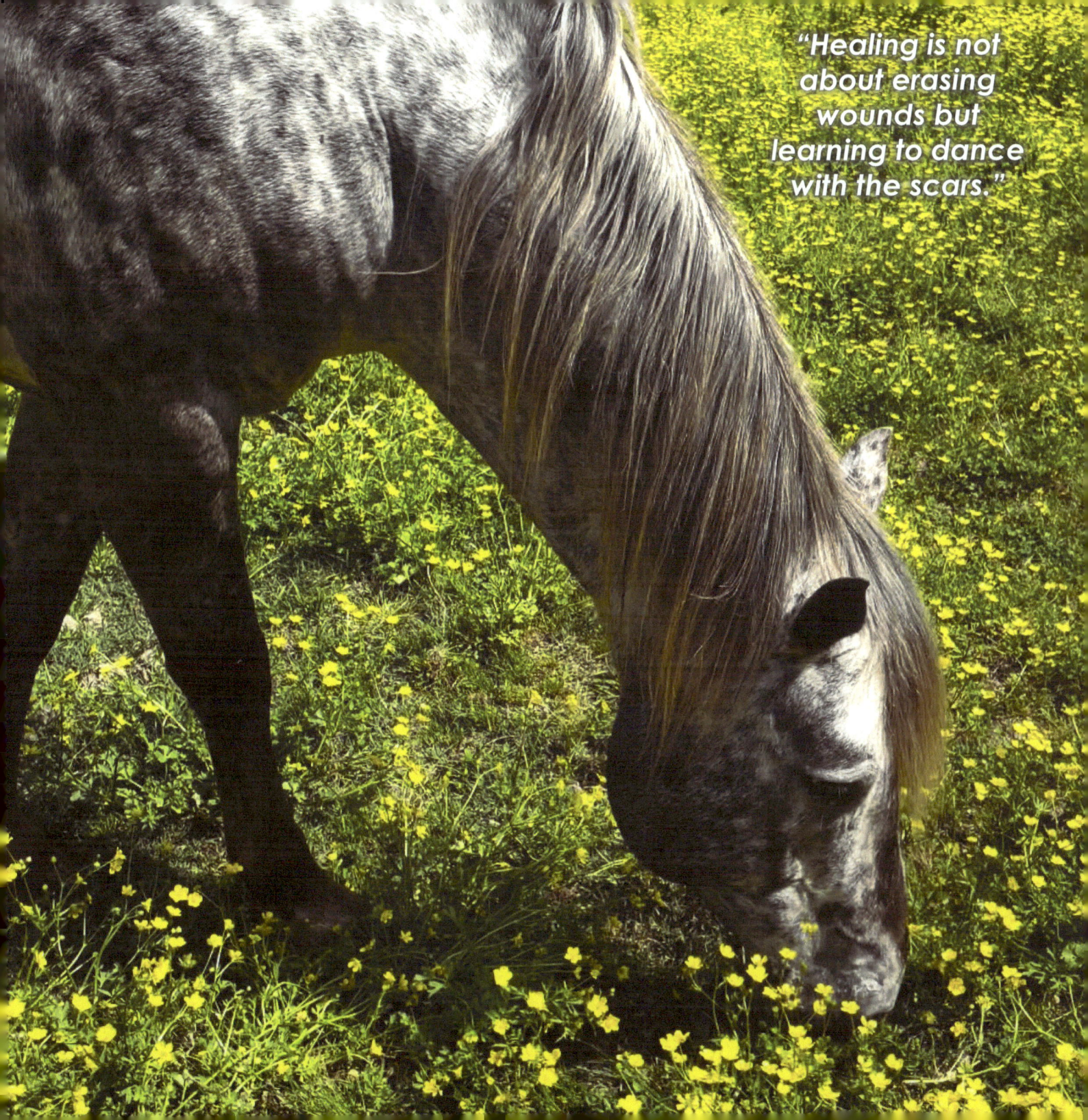

"Healing is not about erasing wounds but learning to dance with the scars."

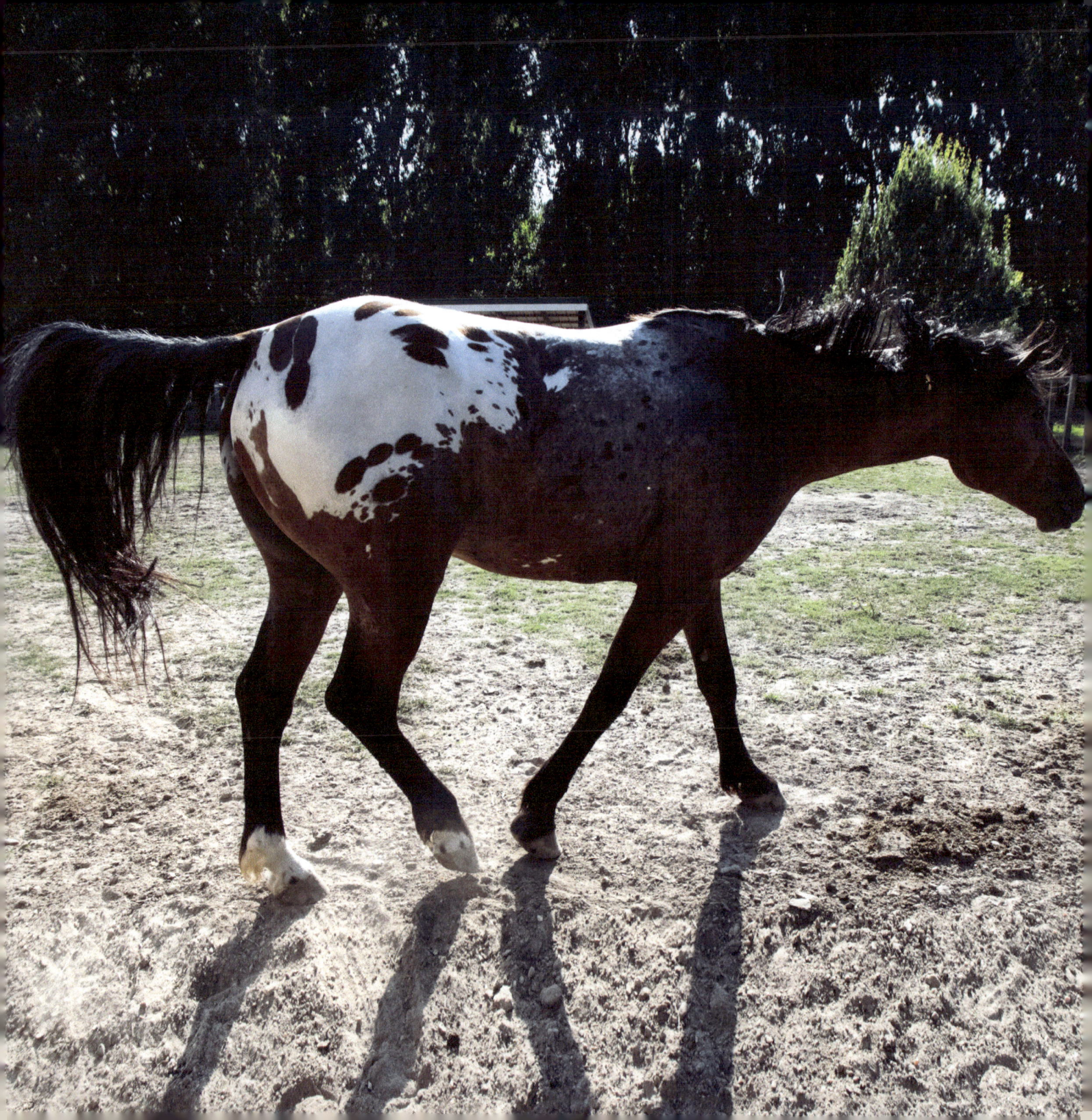

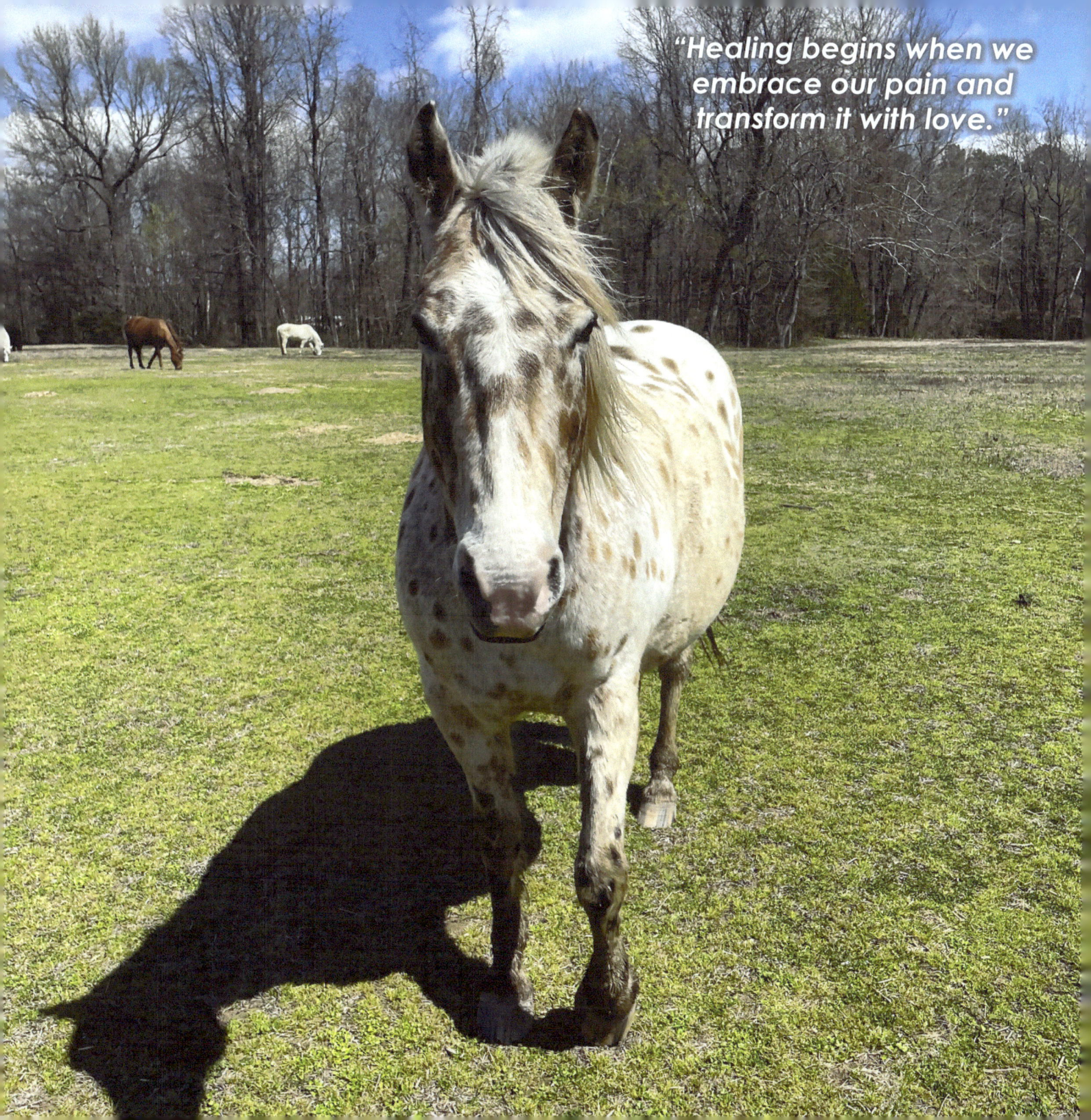

"Healing begins when we embrace our pain and transform it with love."

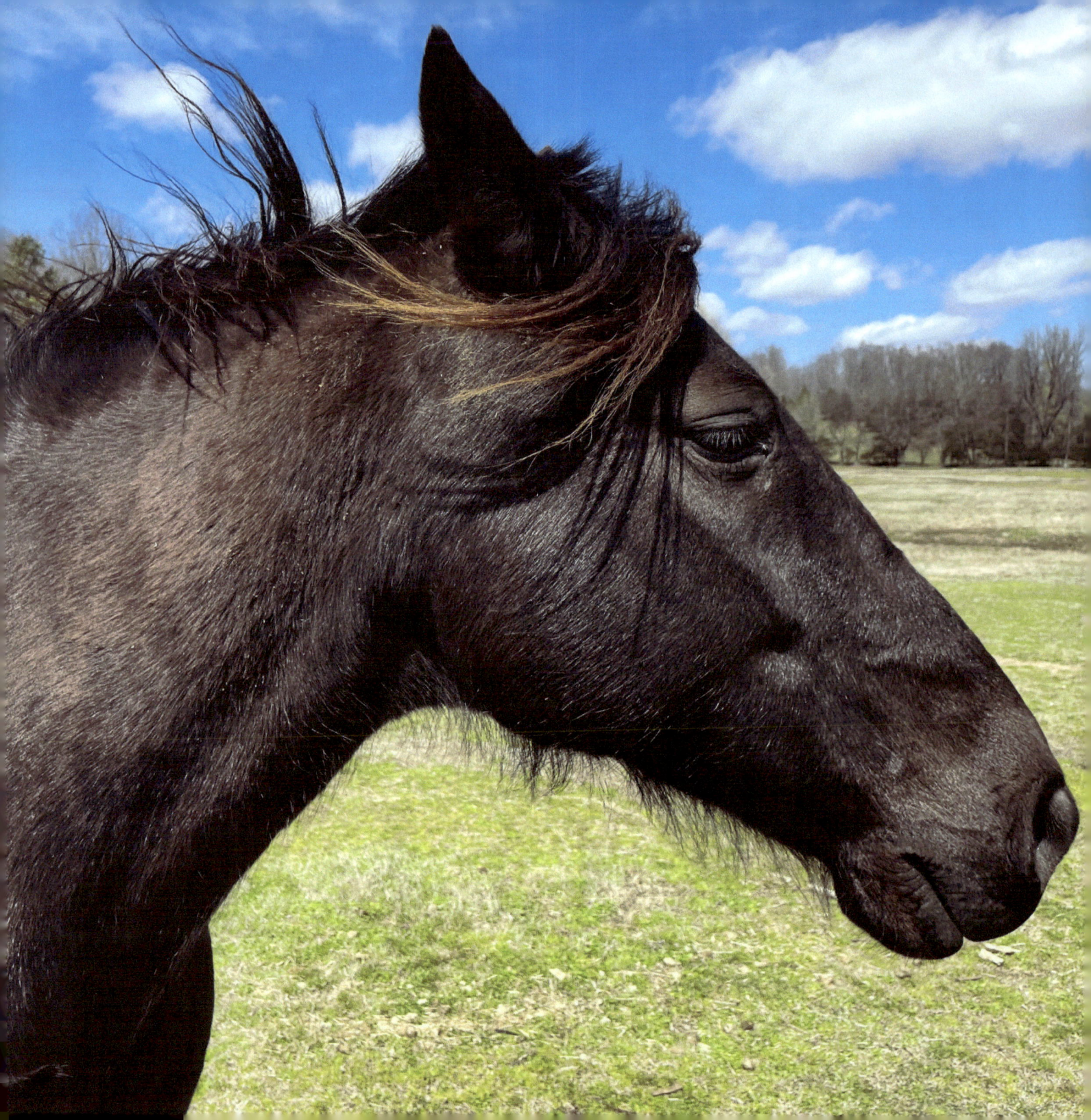

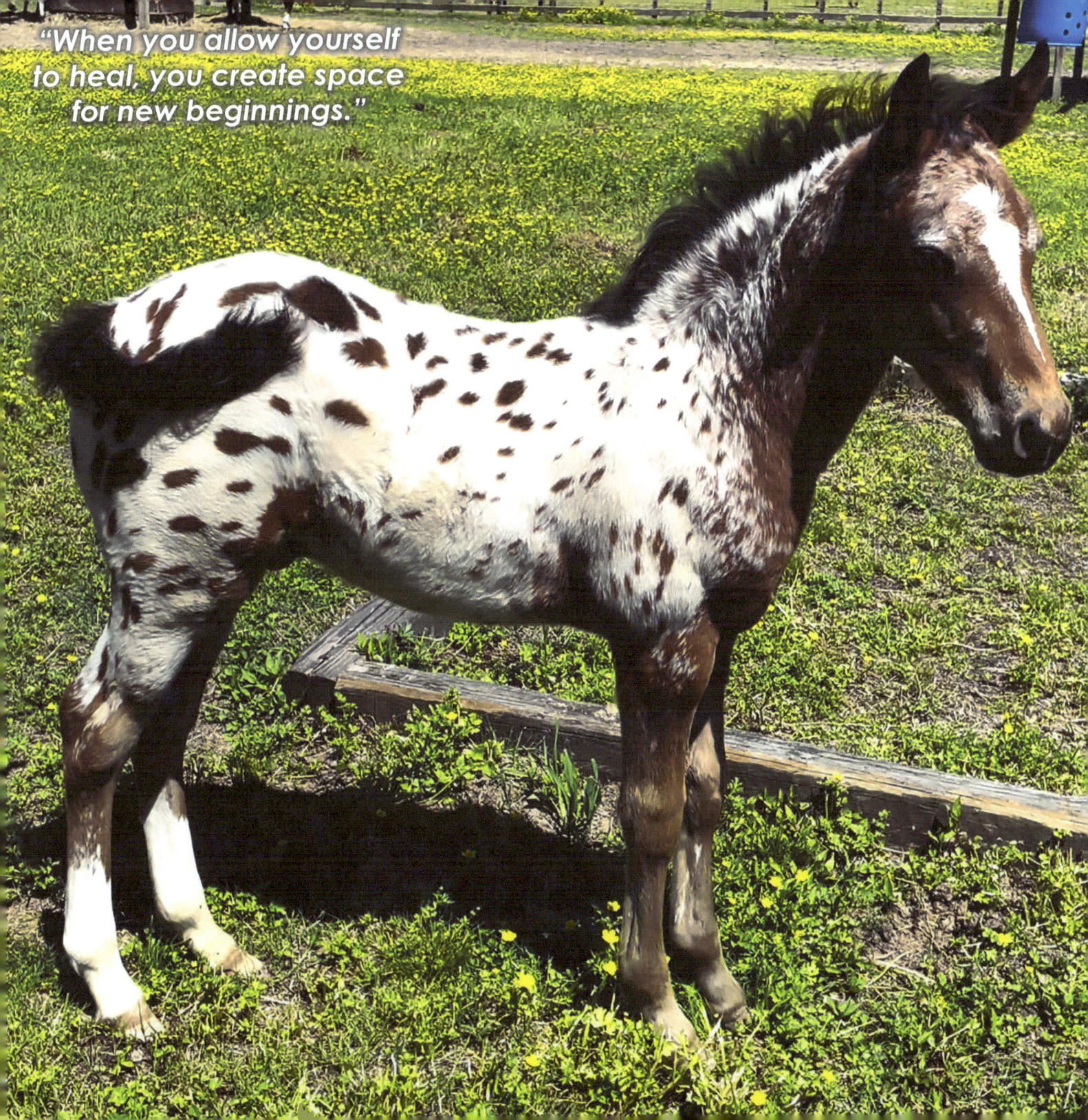

"When you allow yourself to heal, you create space for new beginnings."

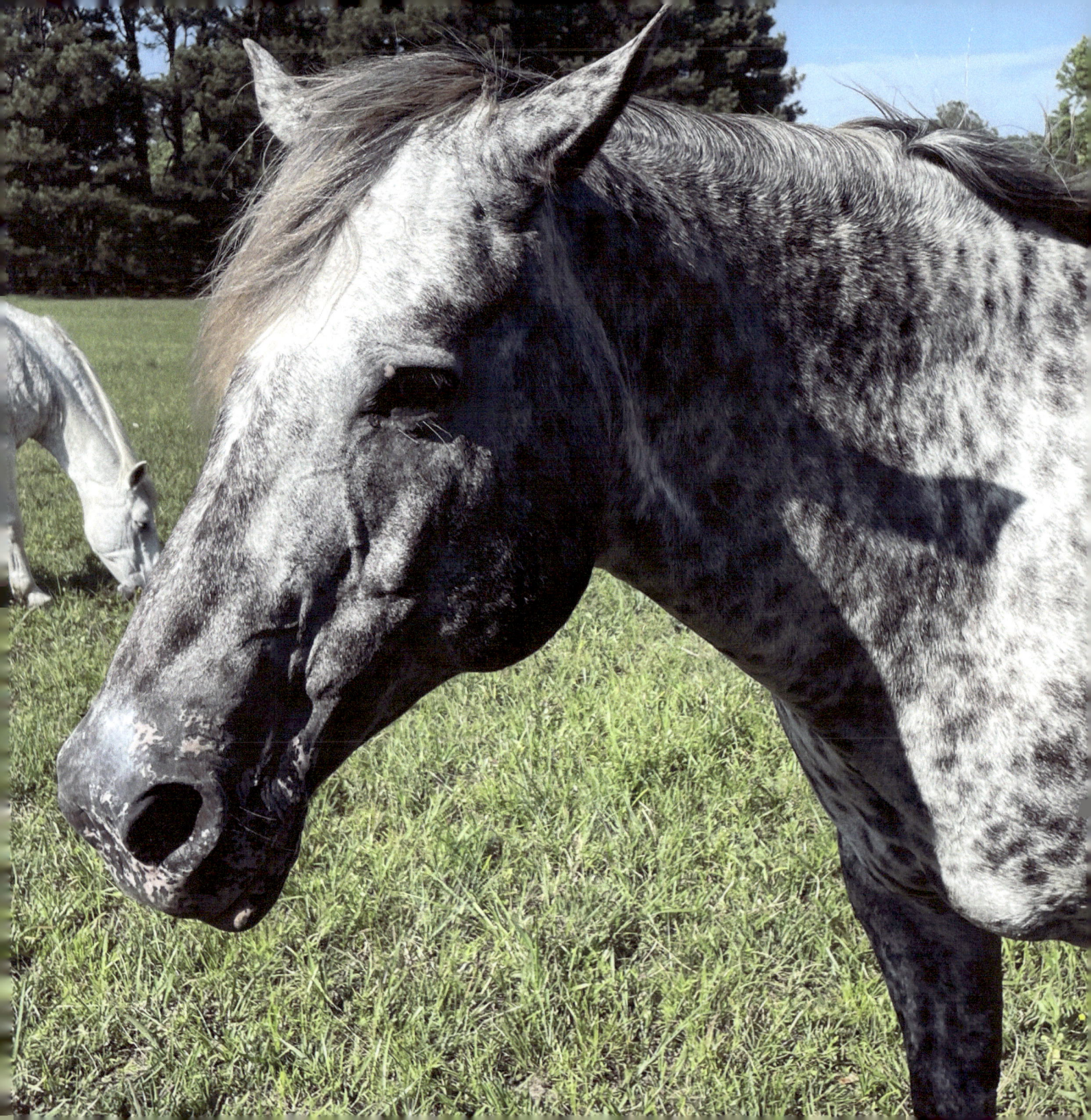

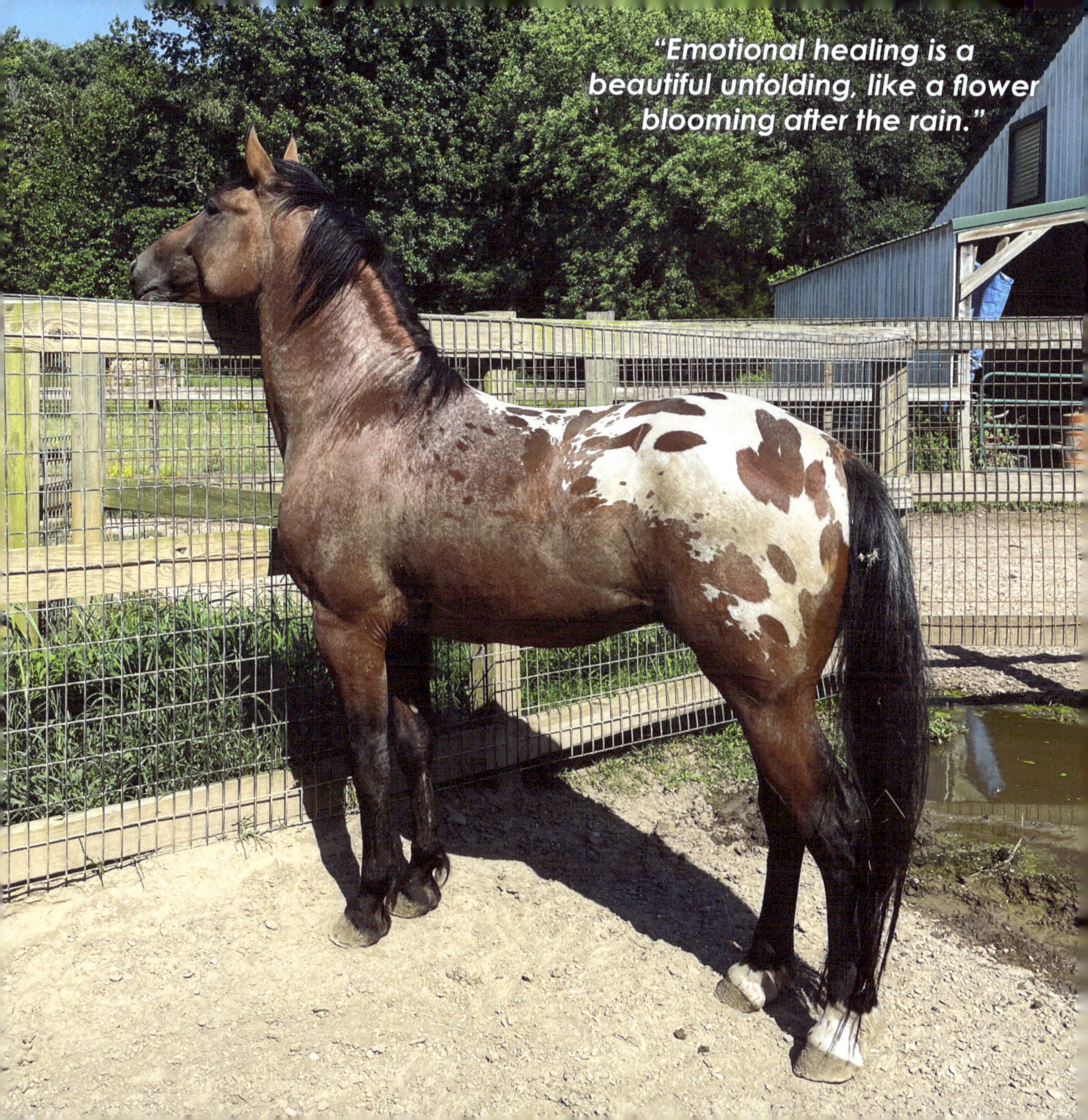

"Emotional healing is a beautiful unfolding, like a flower blooming after the rain."

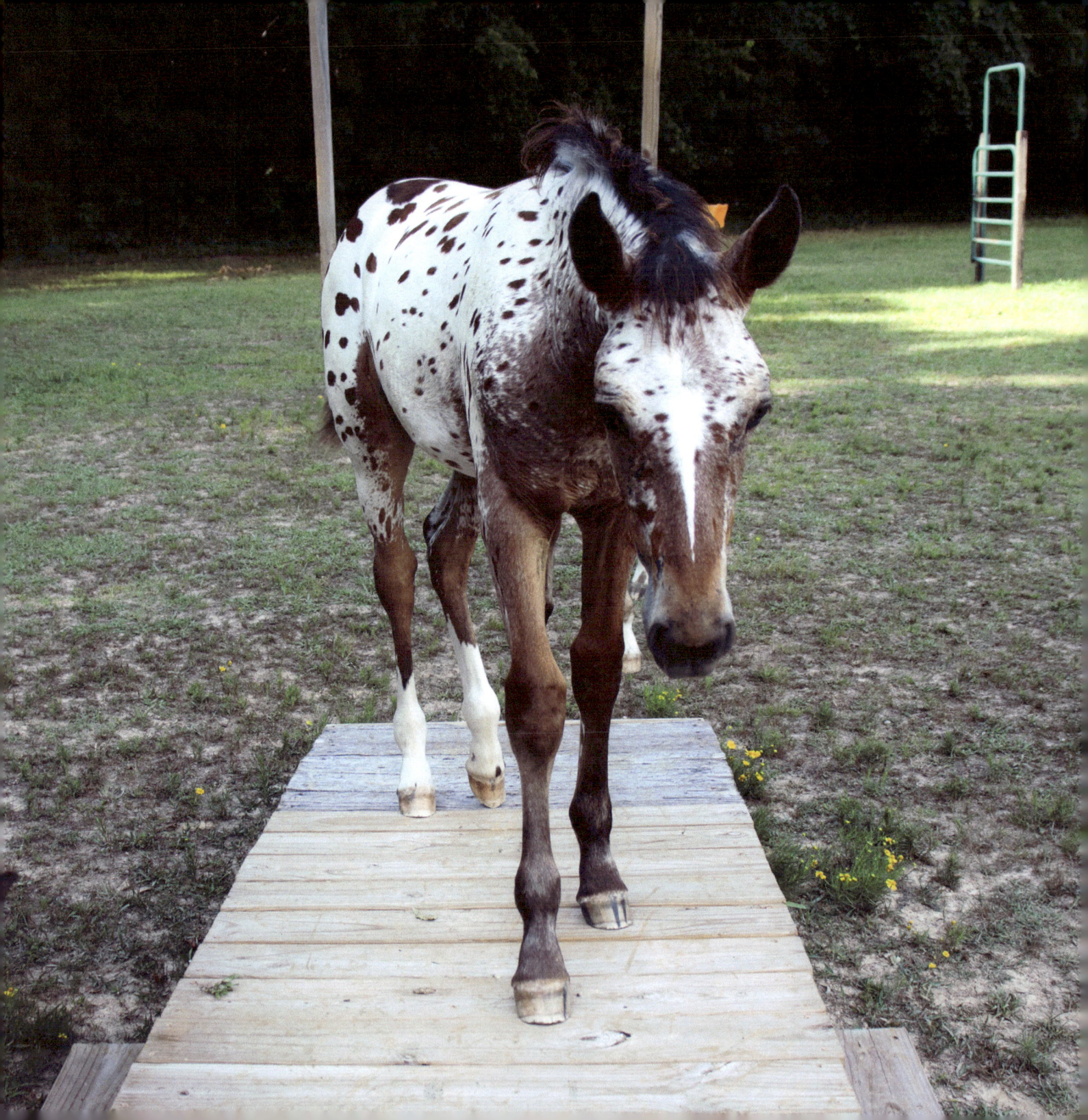

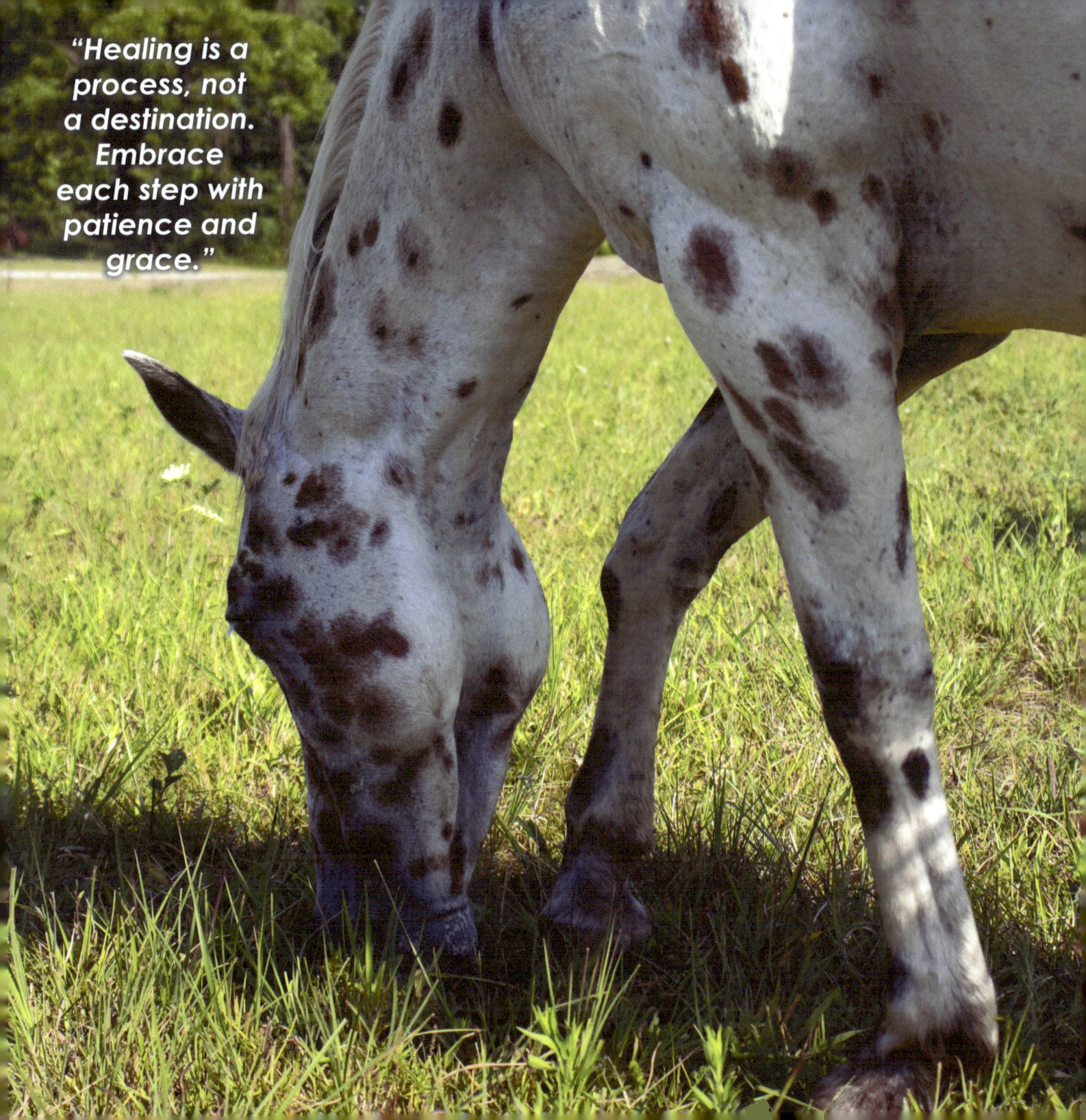

"Healing is a process, not a destination. Embrace each step with patience and grace."

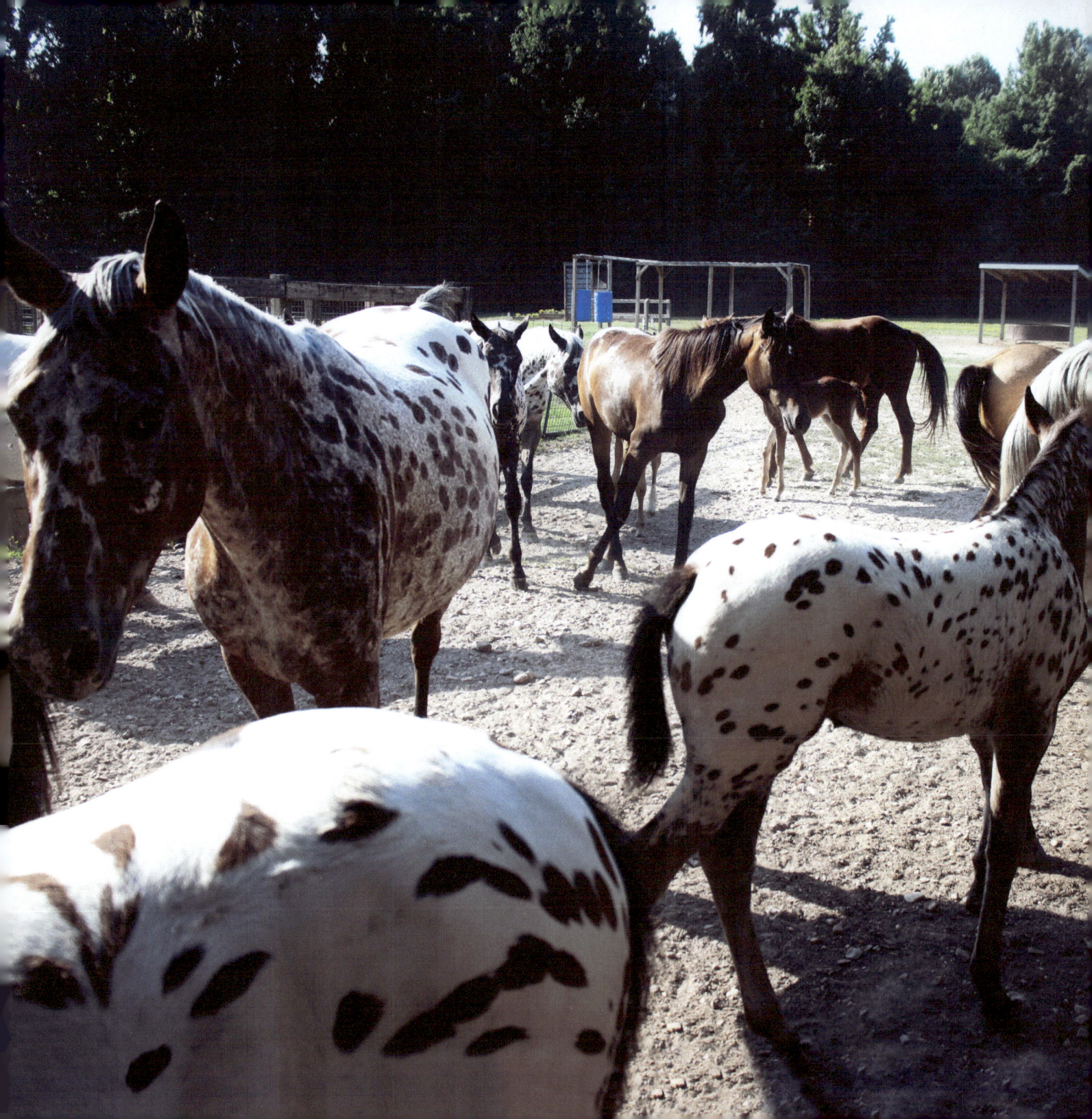

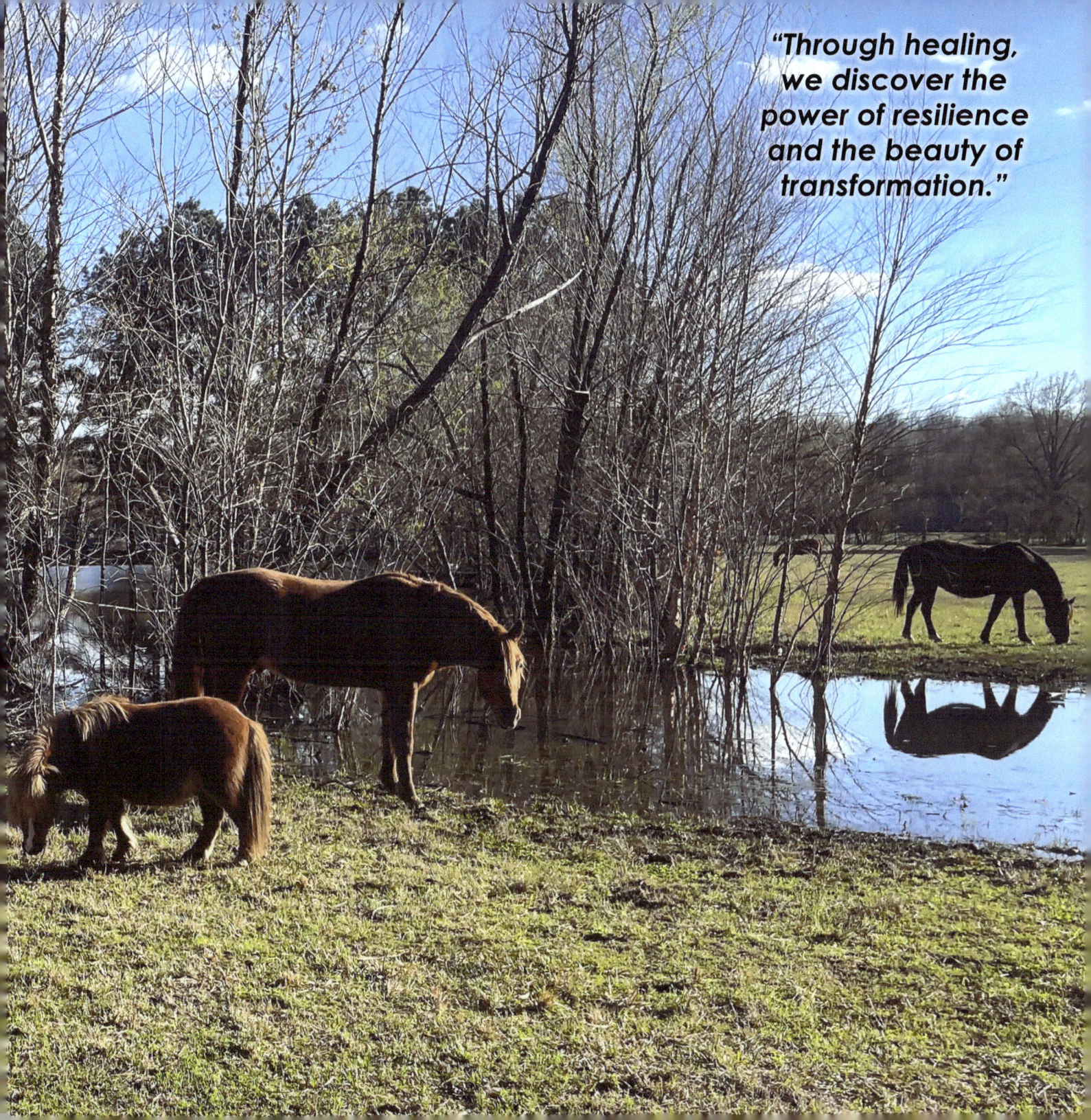

"Through healing, we discover the power of resilience and the beauty of transformation."

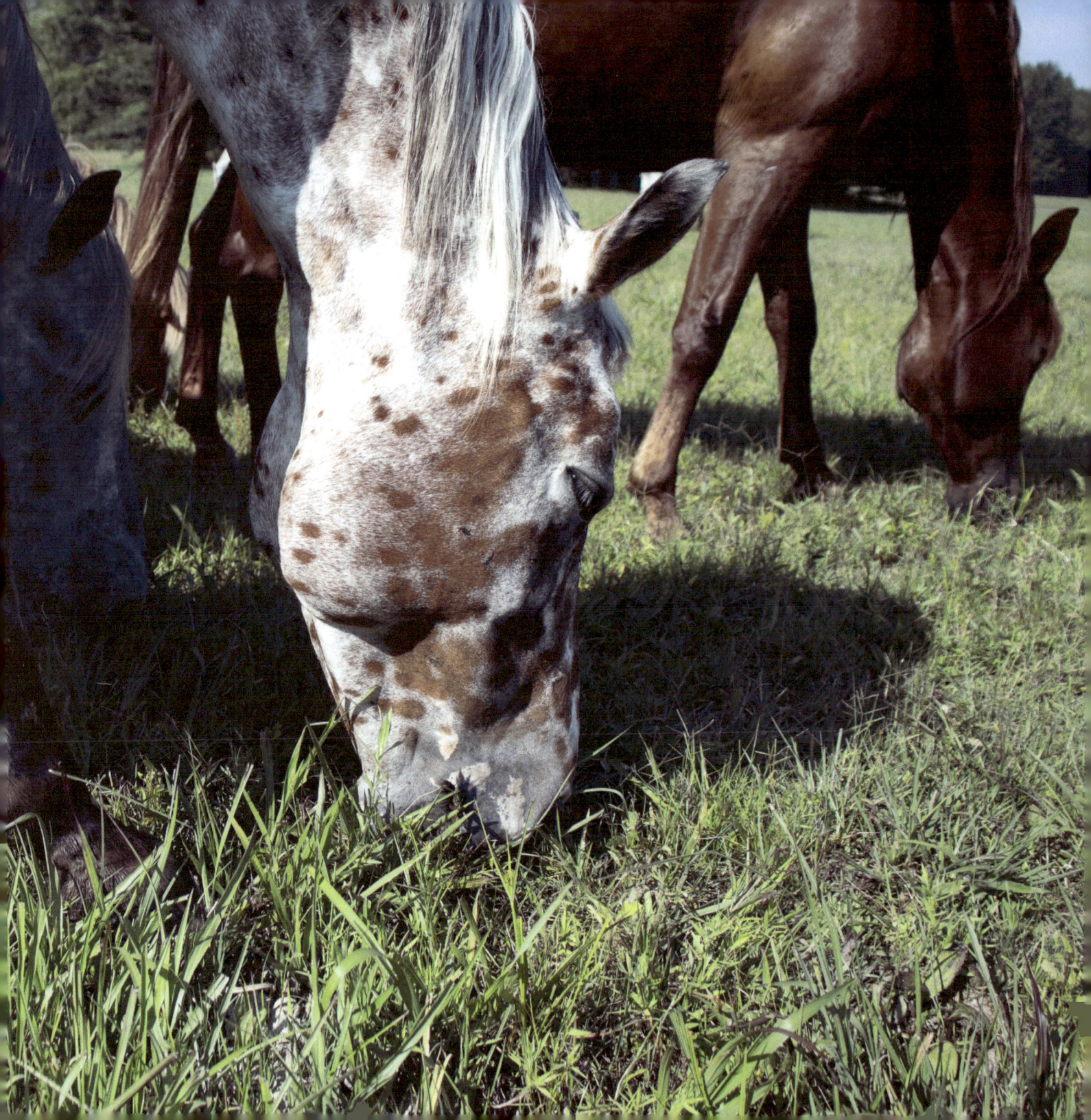

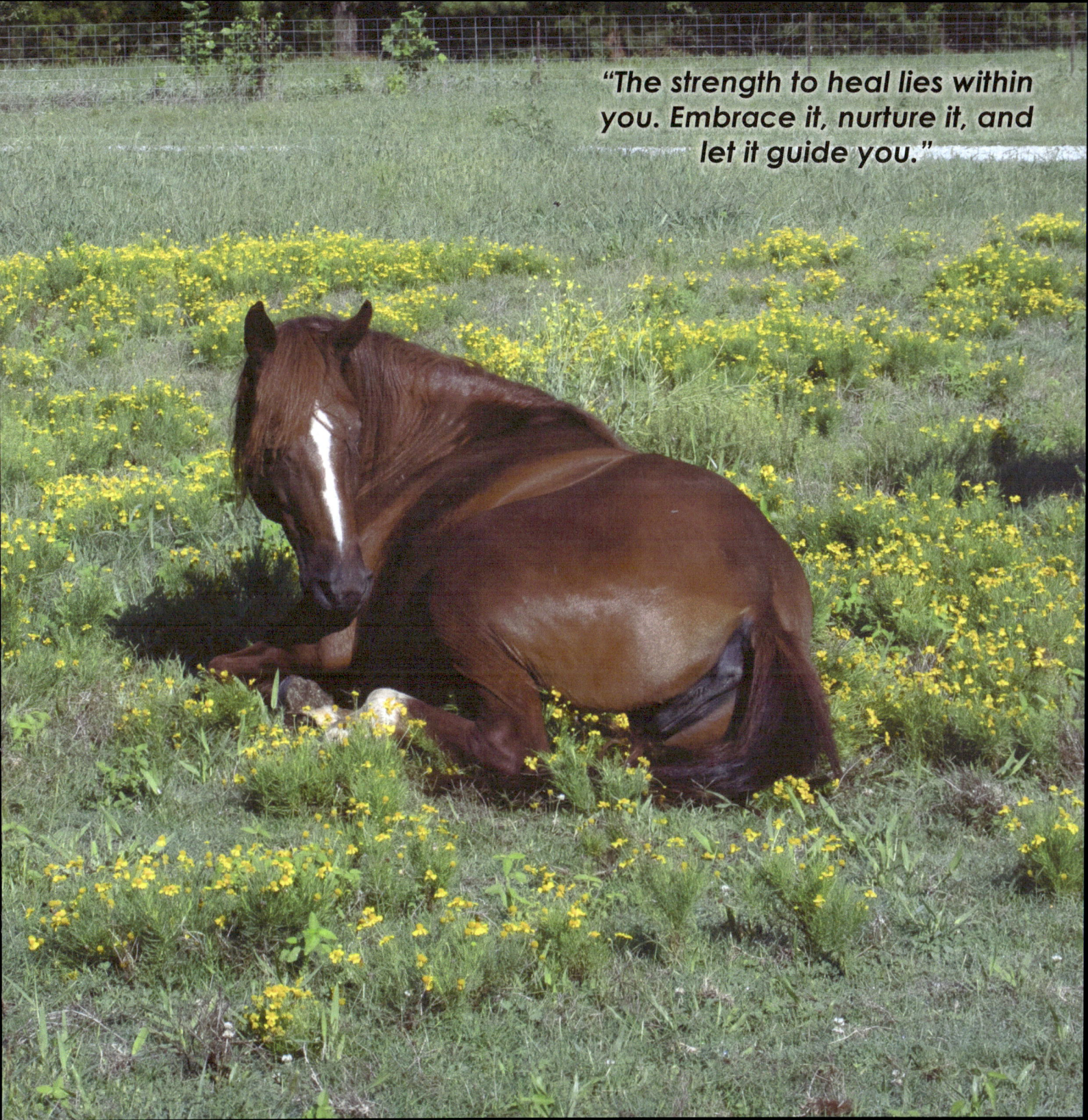

"The strength to heal lies within you. Embrace it, nurture it, and let it guide you."

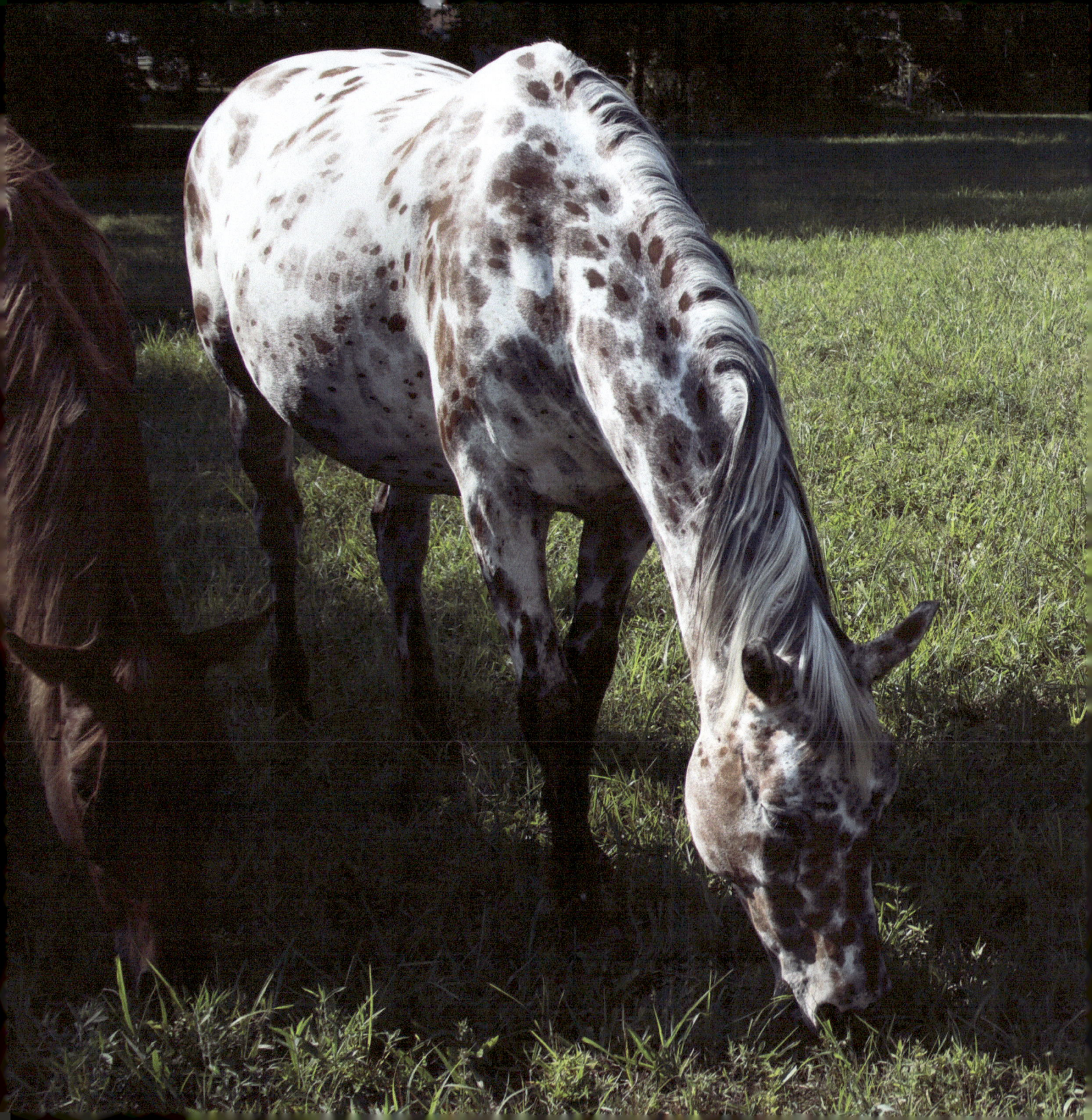

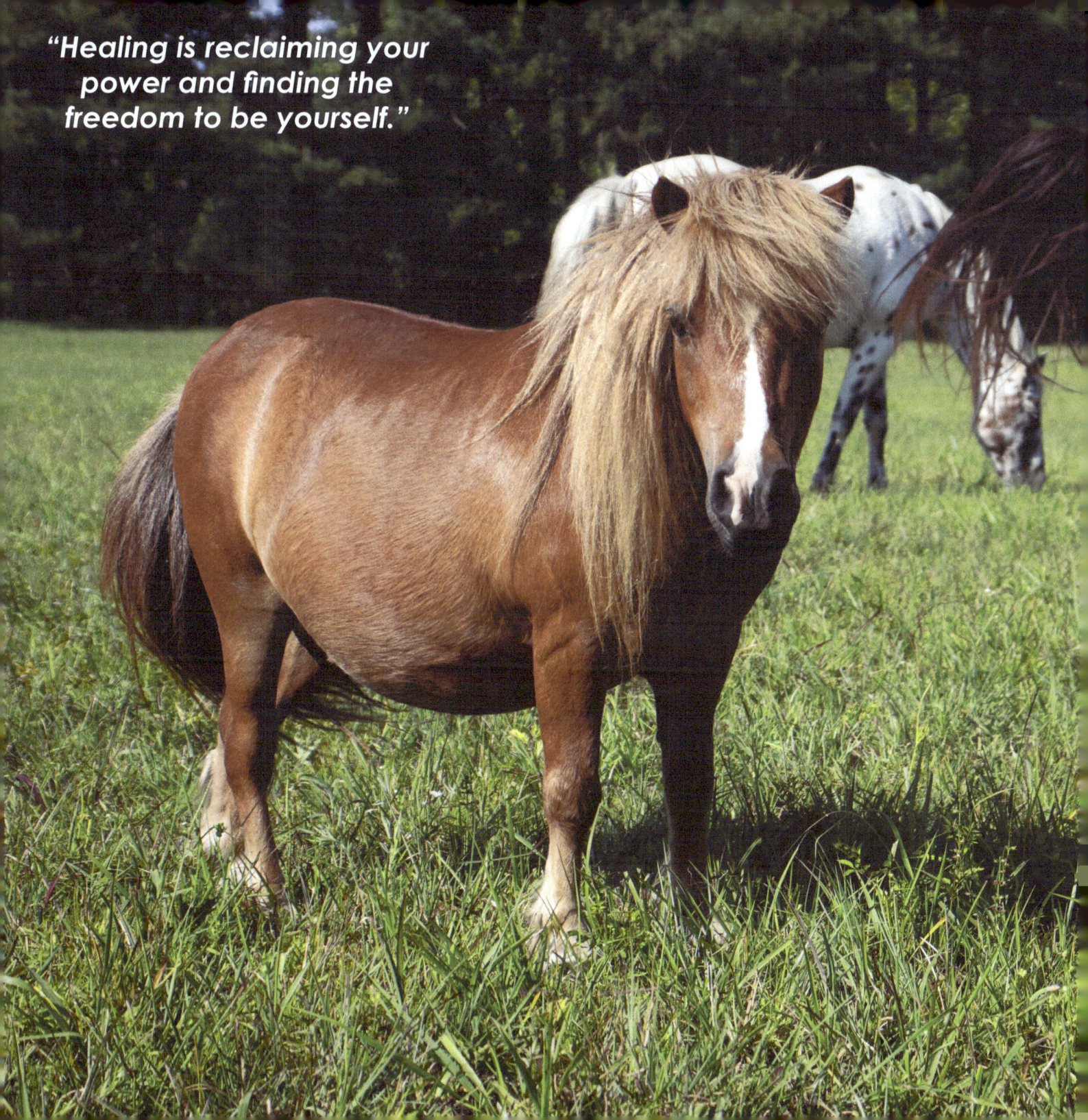

"Healing is reclaiming your power and finding the freedom to be yourself."

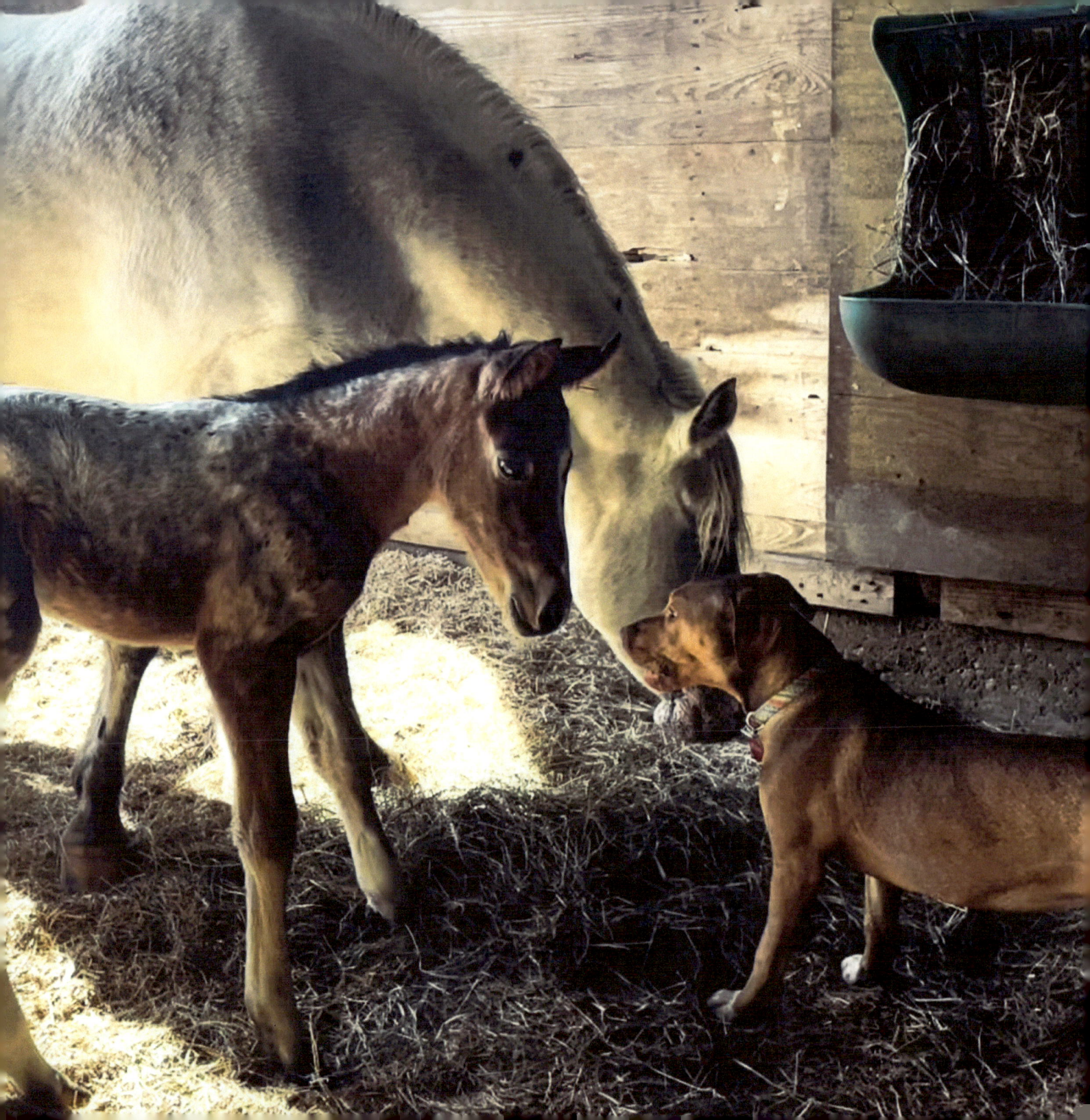

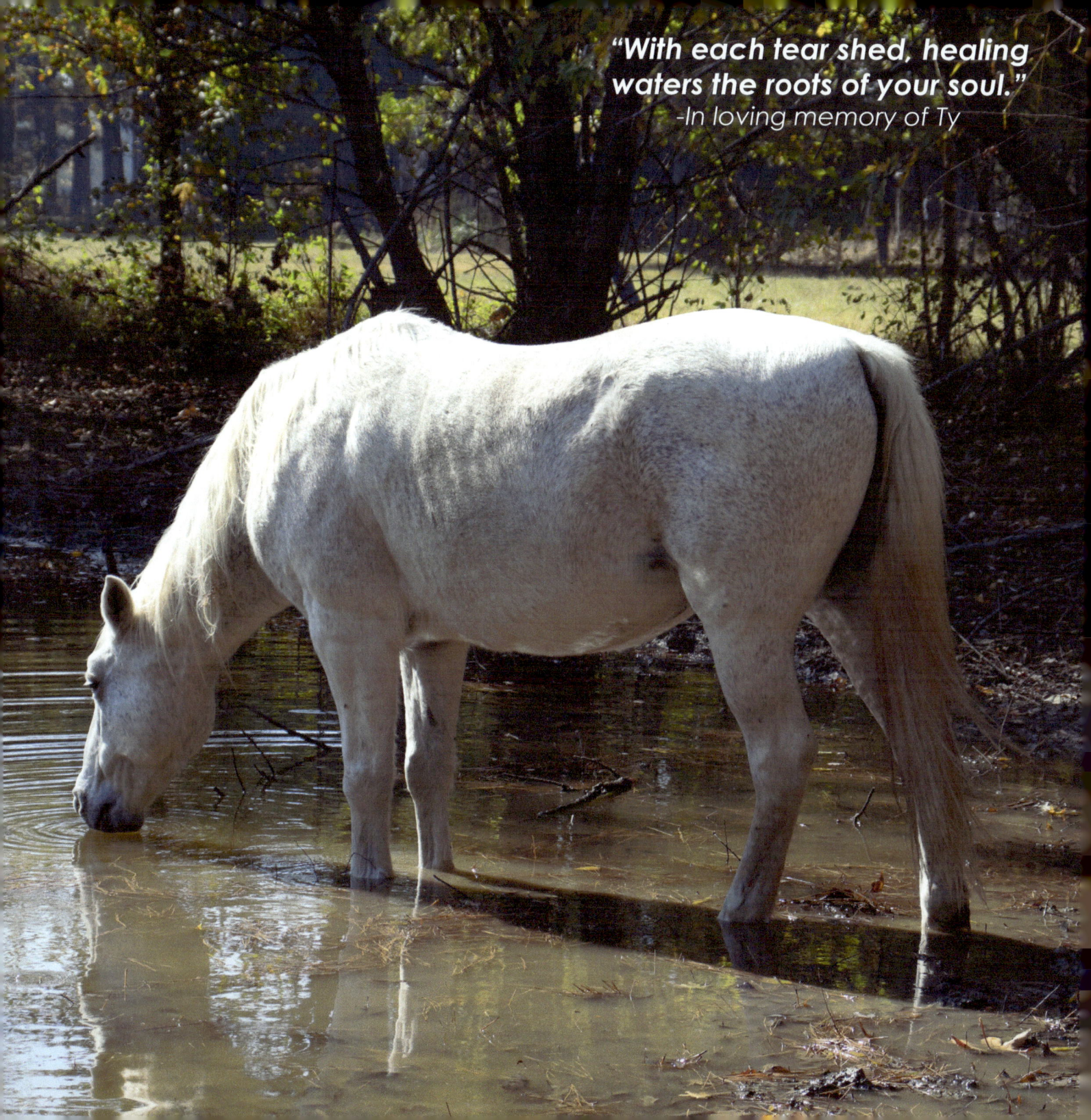

"With each tear shed, healing waters the roots of your soul."
-In loving memory of Ty

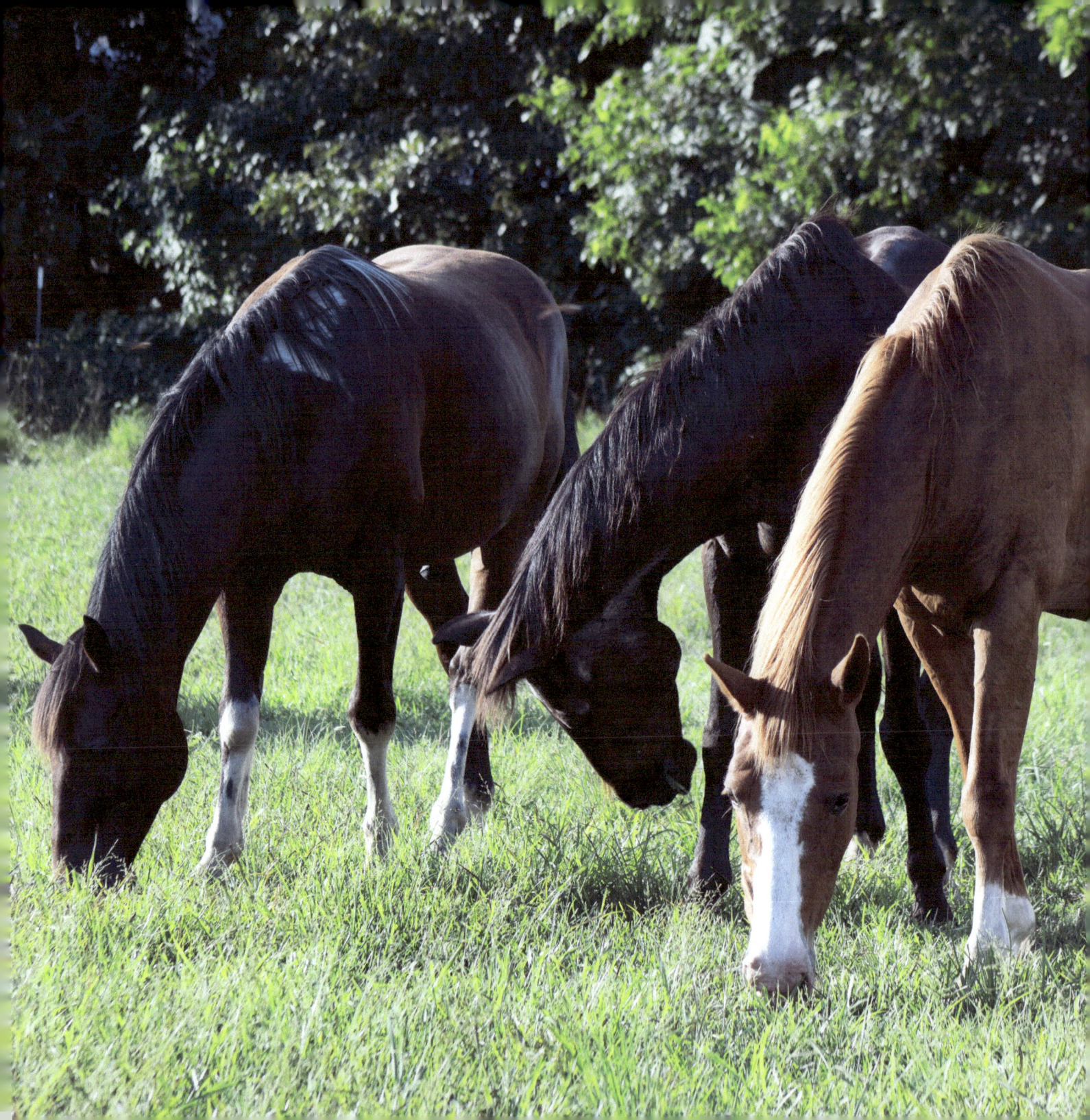

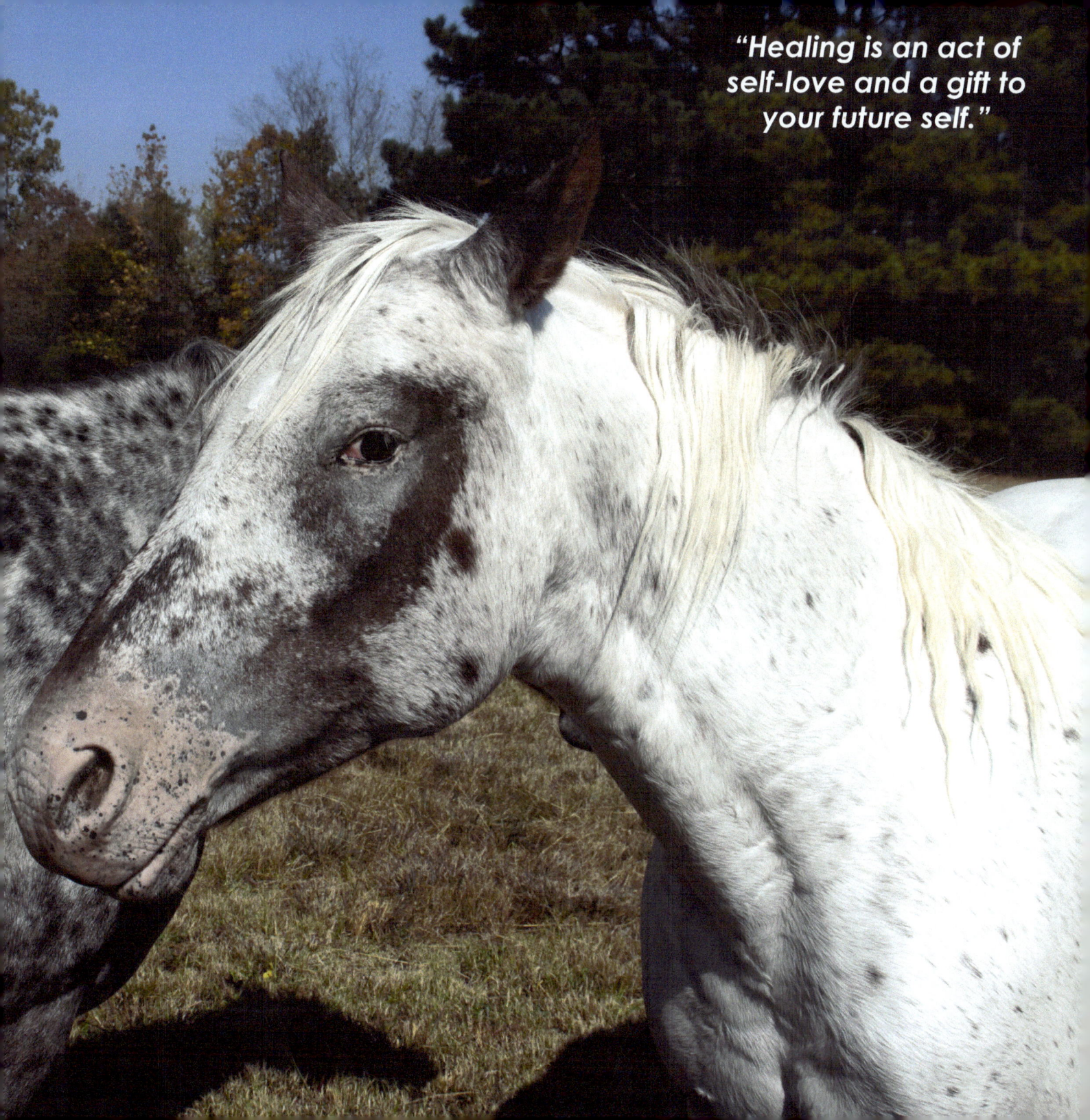

"Healing is an act of self-love and a gift to your future self."

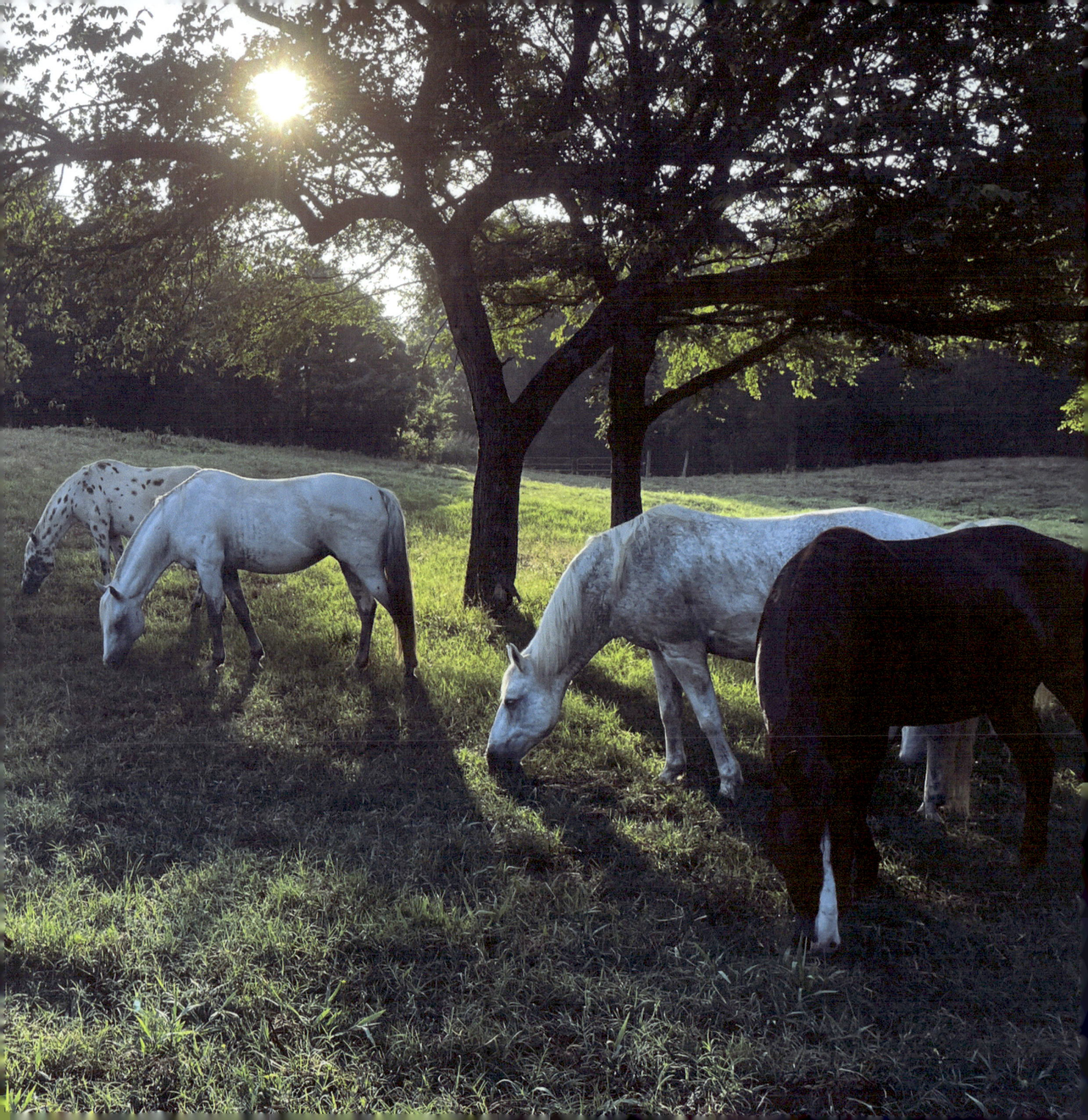

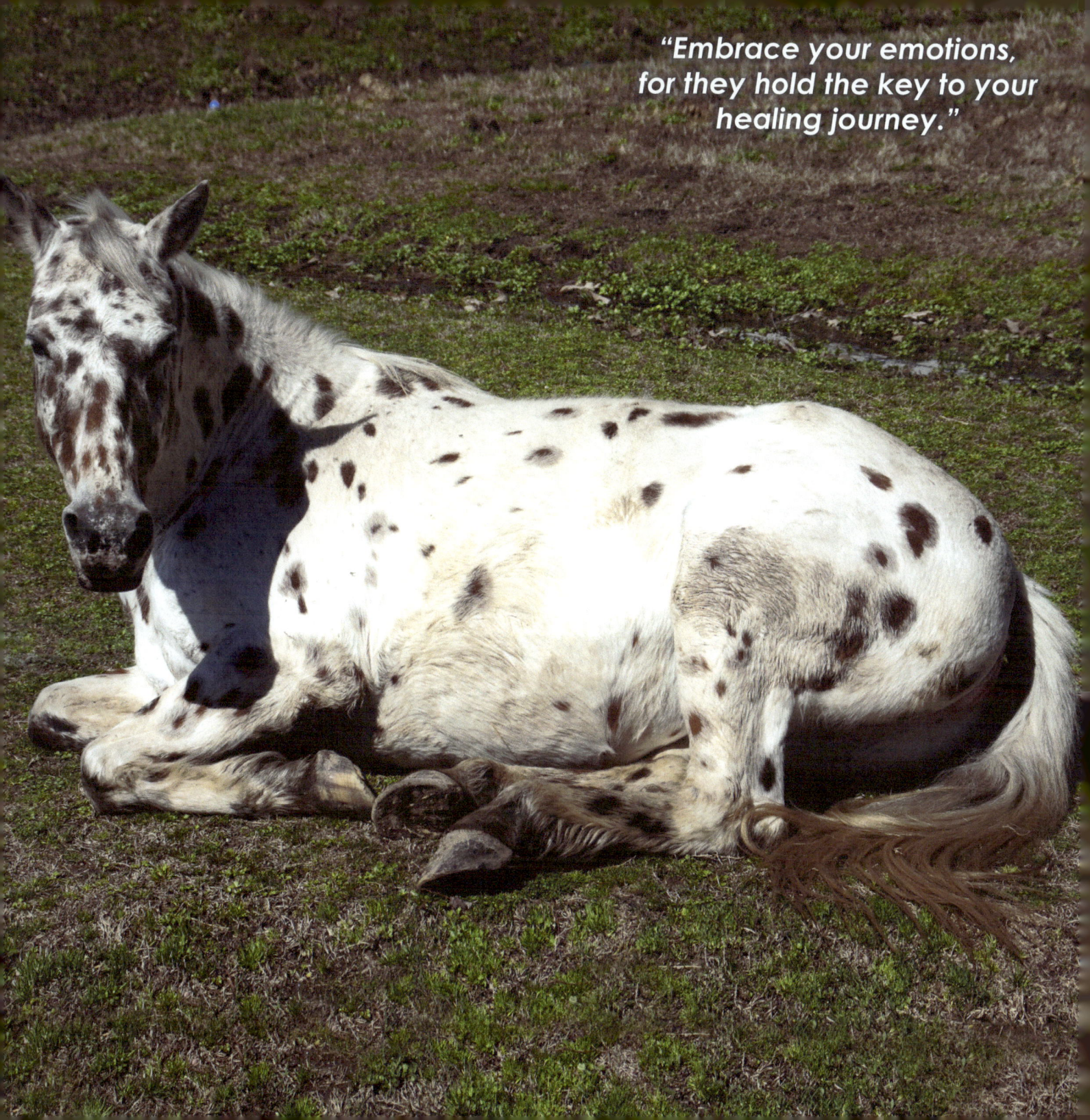

"Embrace your emotions, for they hold the key to your healing journey."

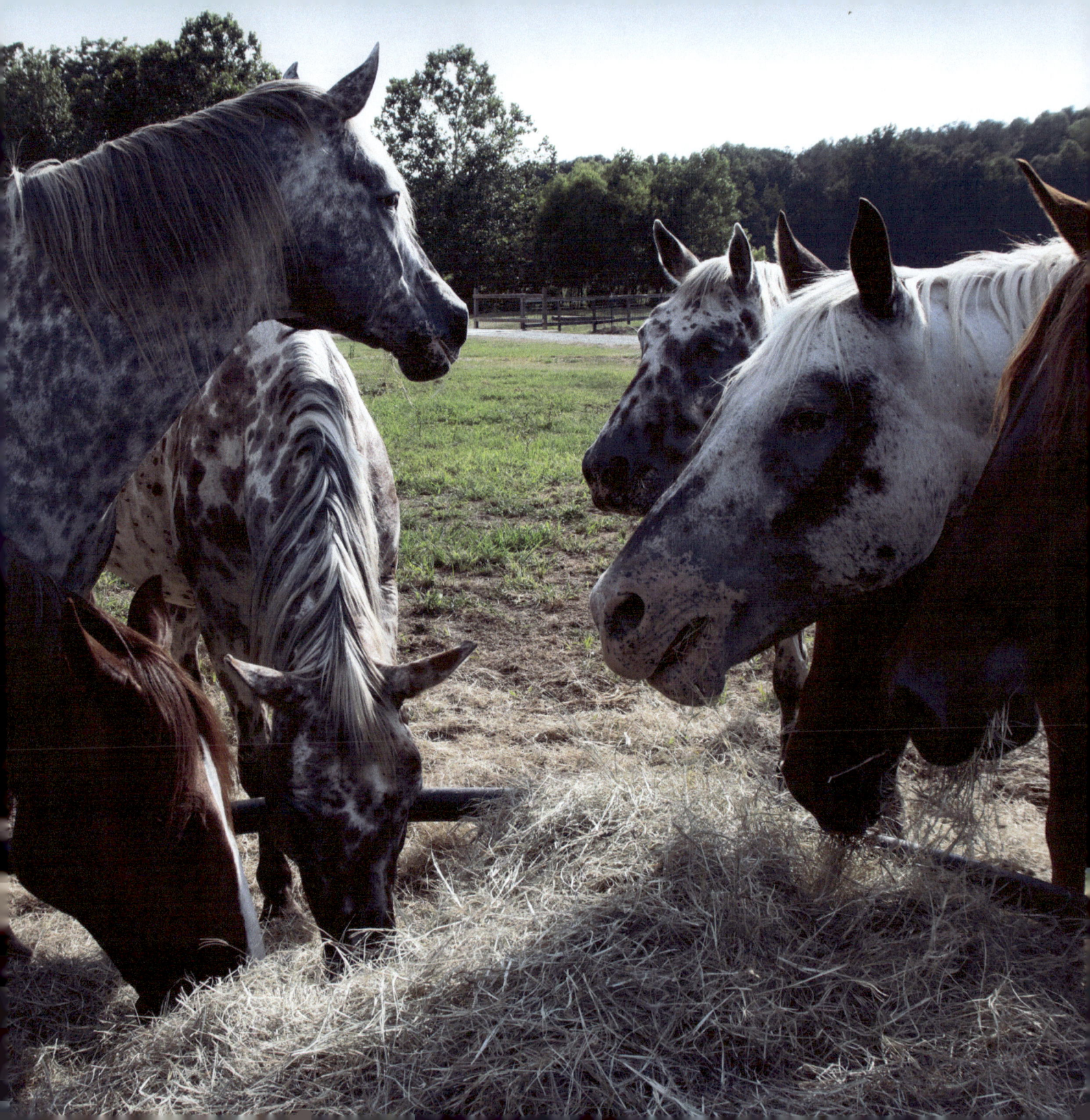

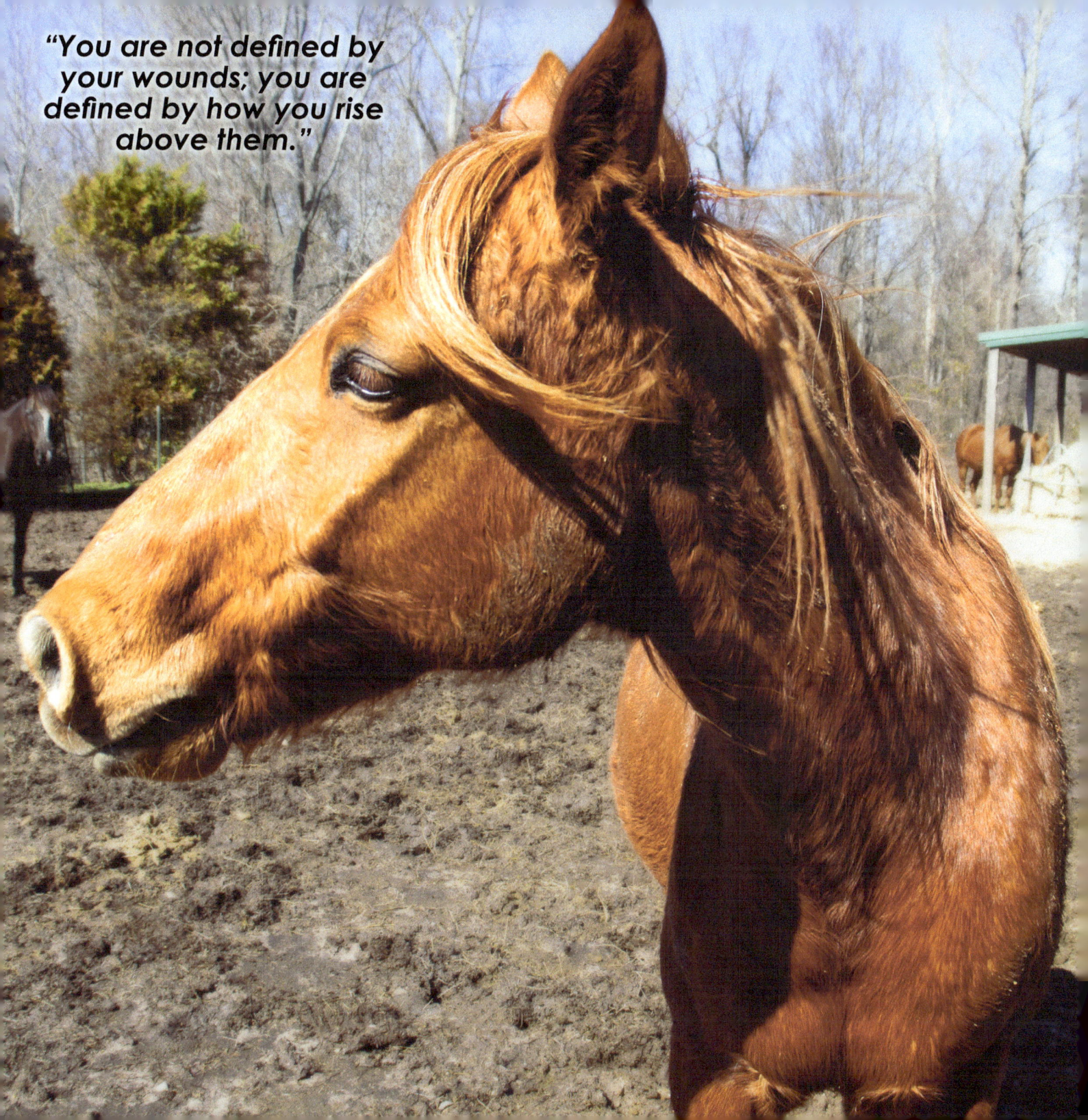

"You are not defined by your wounds; you are defined by how you rise above them."

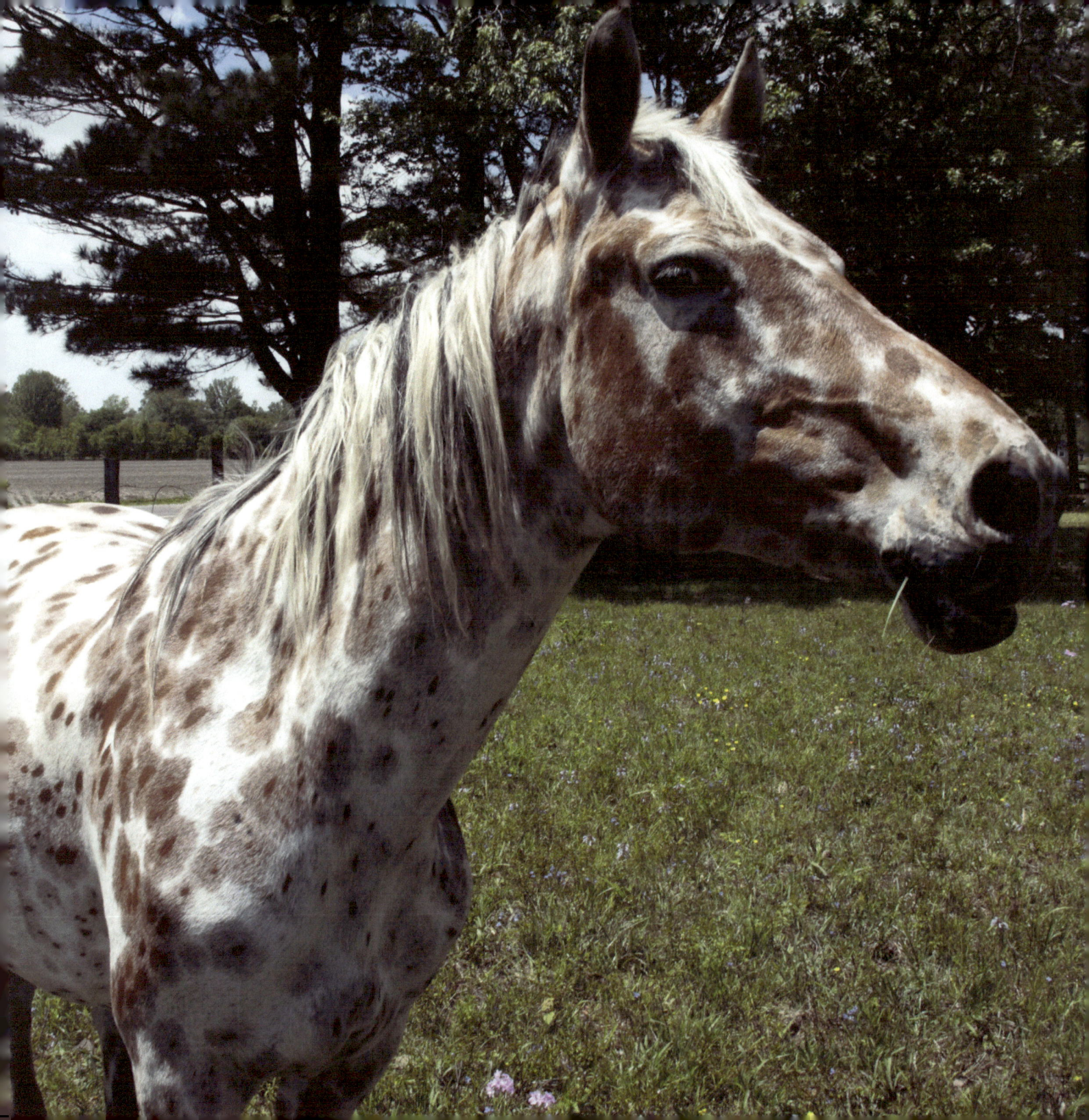

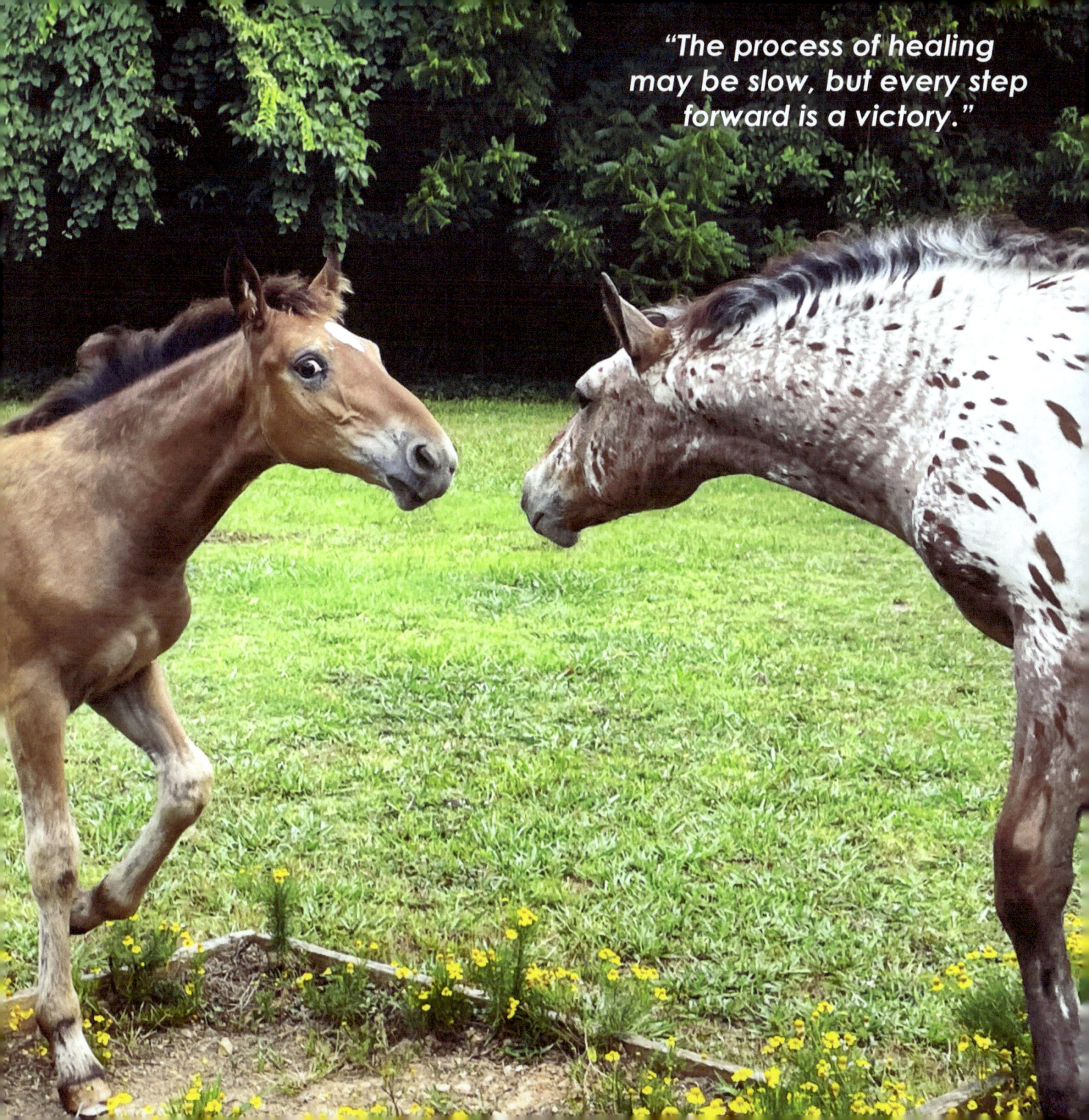

"The process of healing may be slow, but every step forward is a victory."

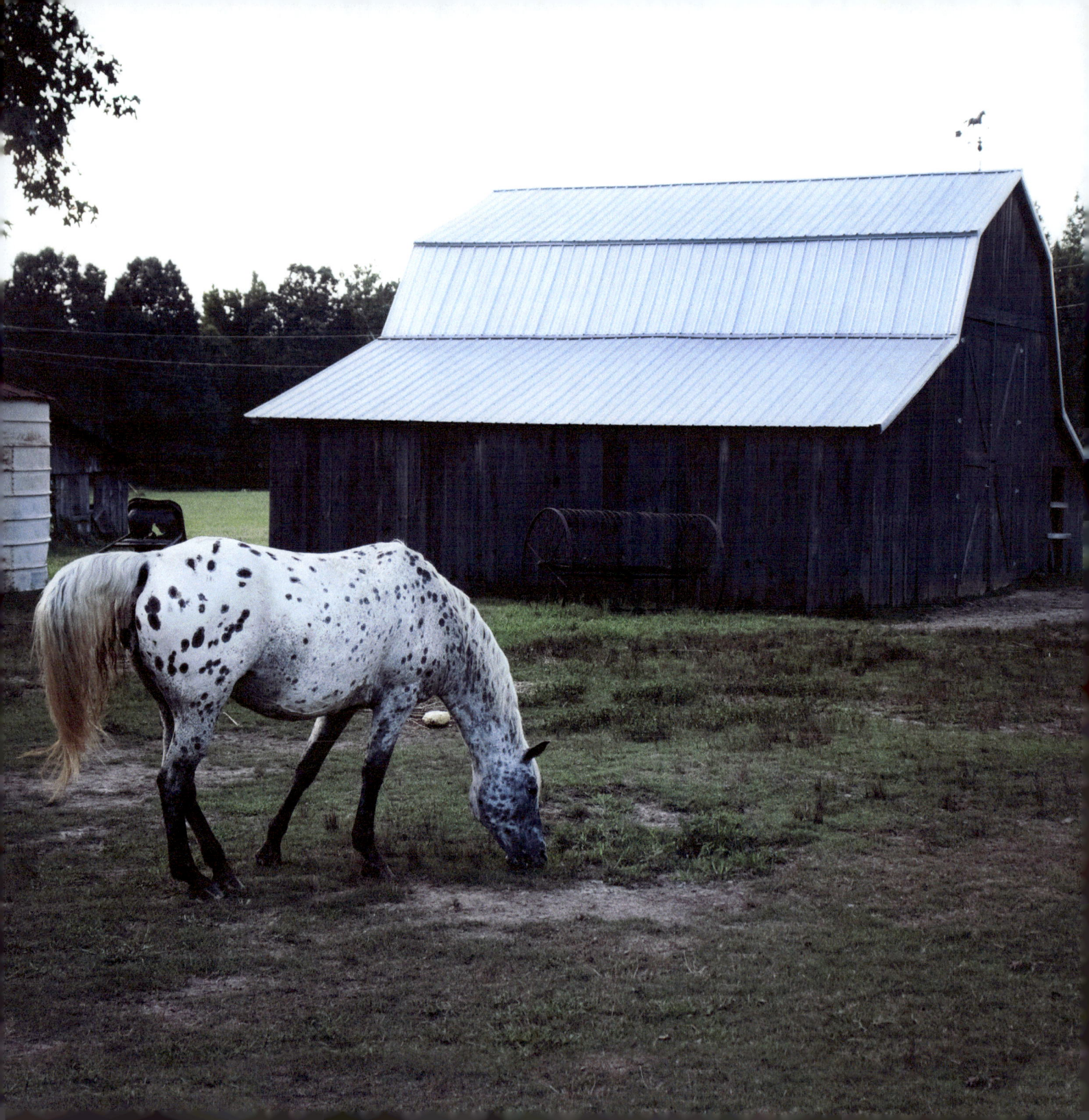

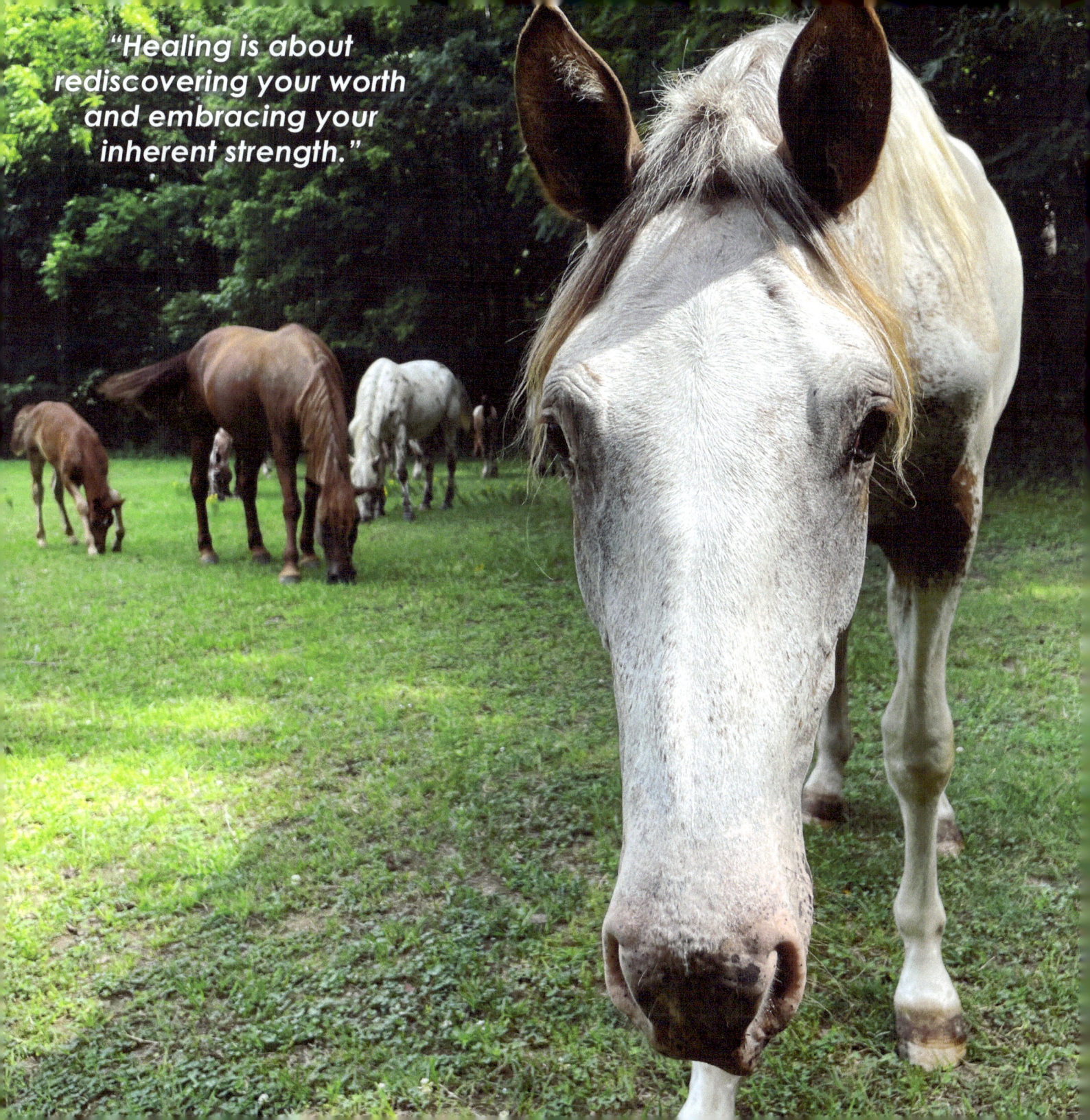

"Healing is about rediscovering your worth and embracing your inherent strength."

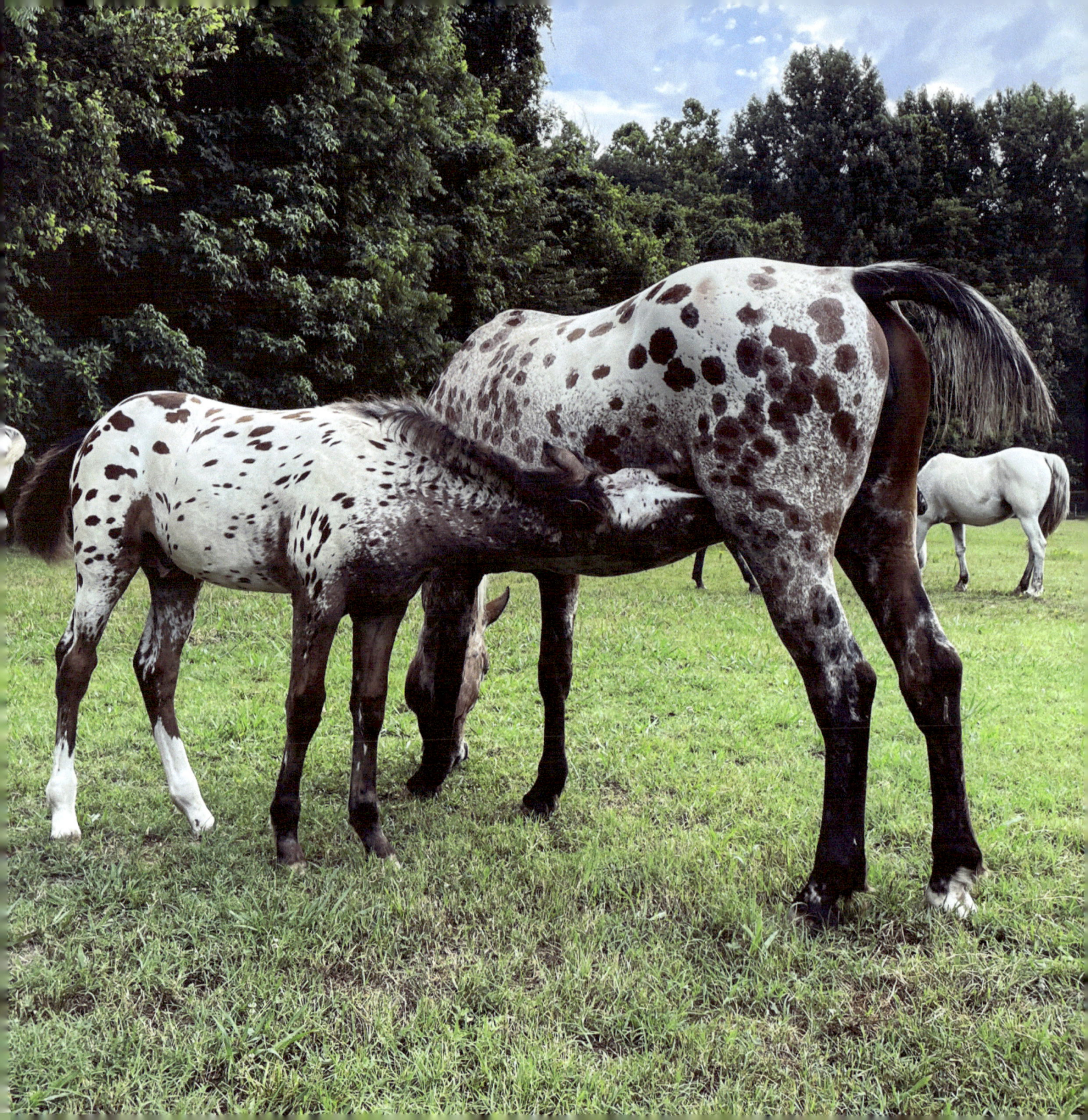

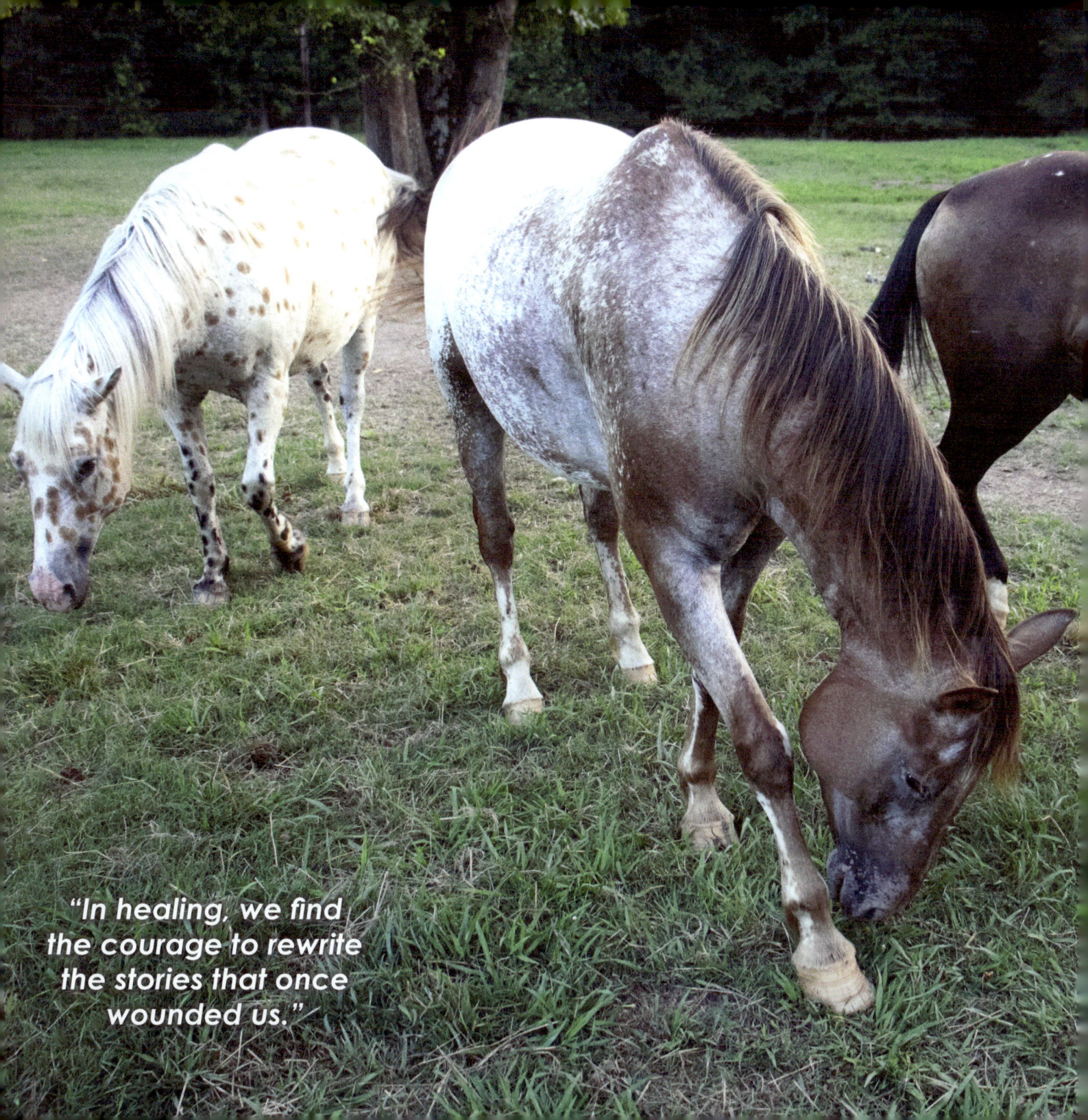

"In healing, we find the courage to rewrite the stories that once wounded us."

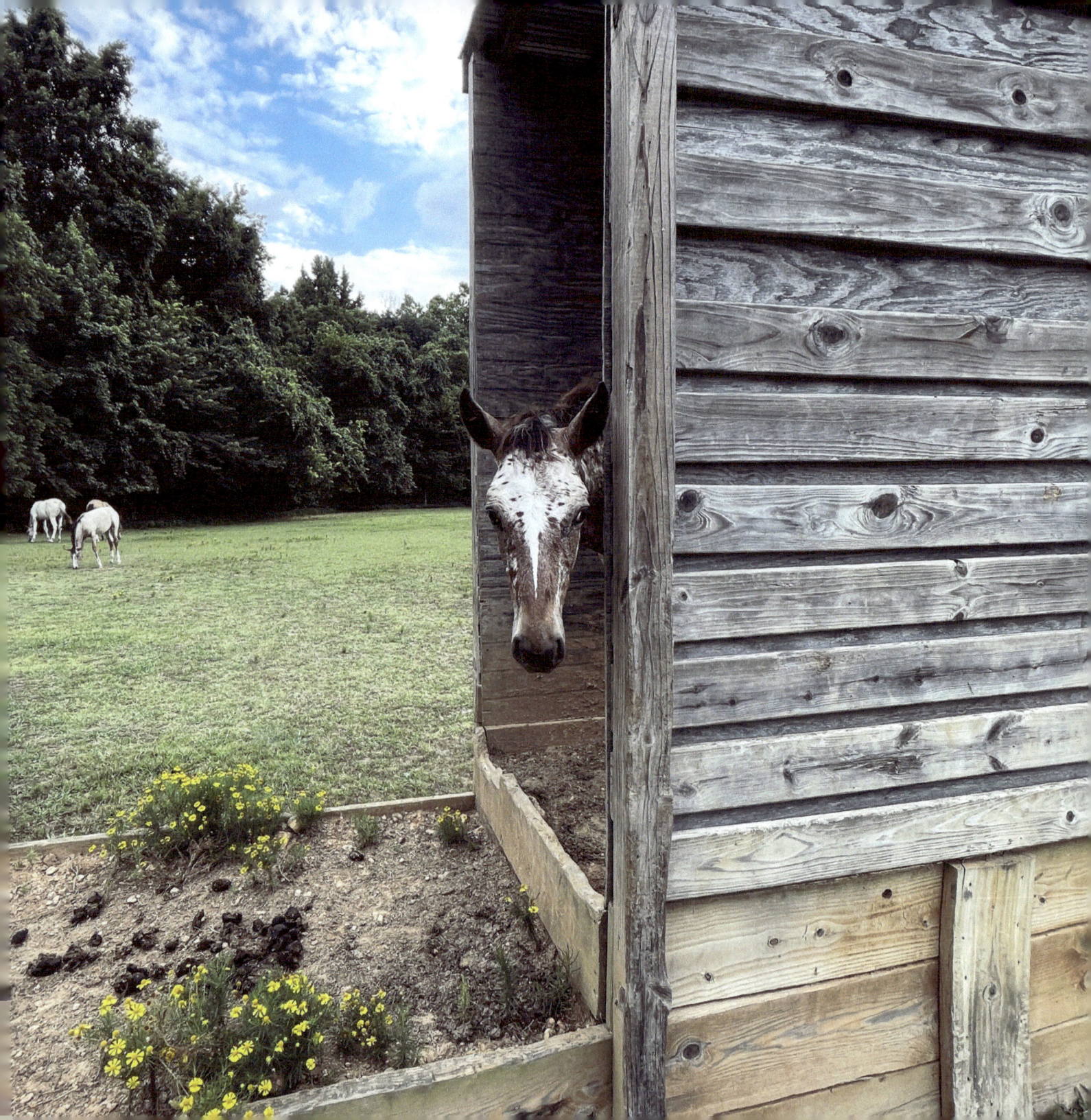

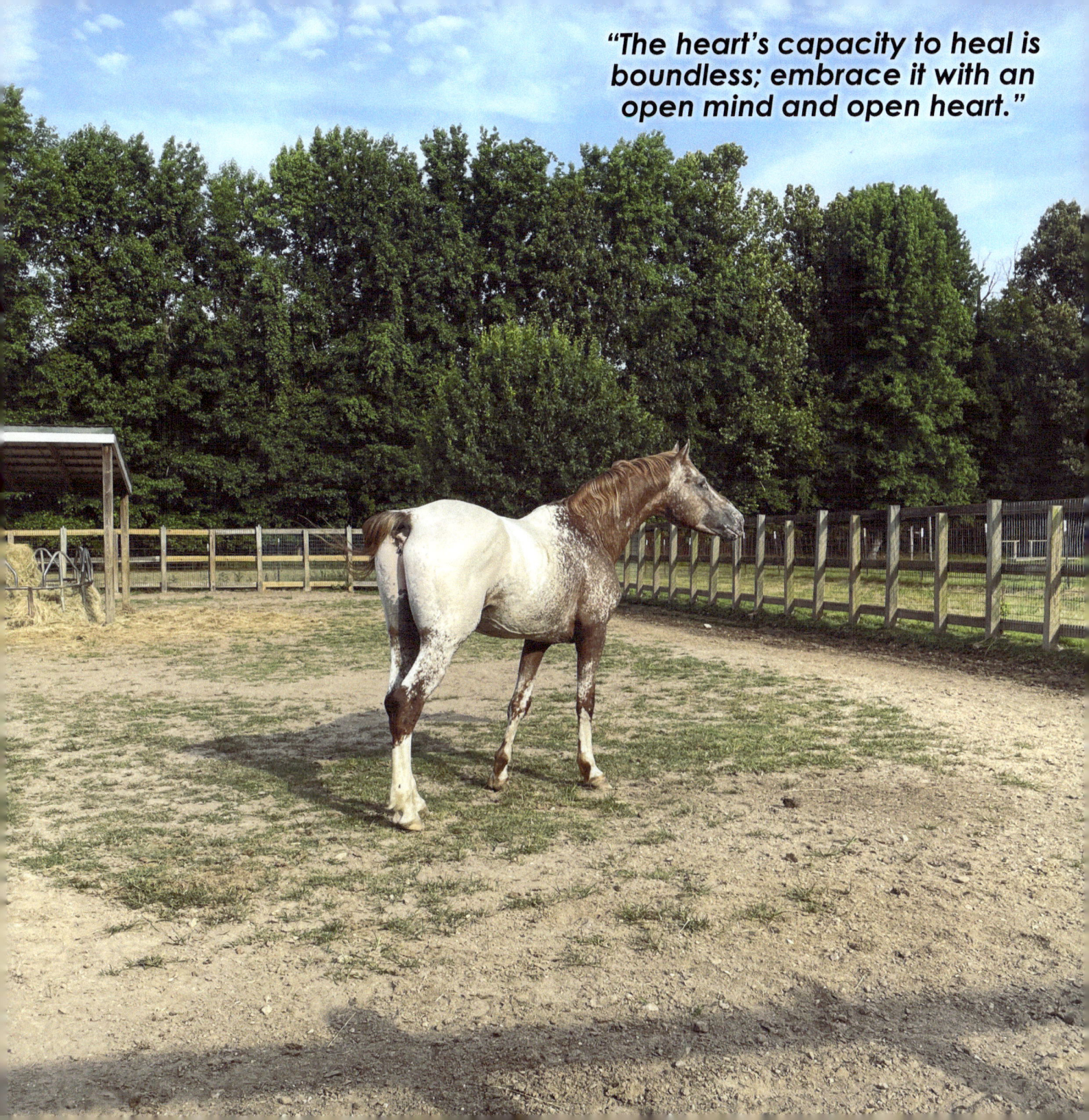

"The heart's capacity to heal is boundless; embrace it with an open mind and open heart."

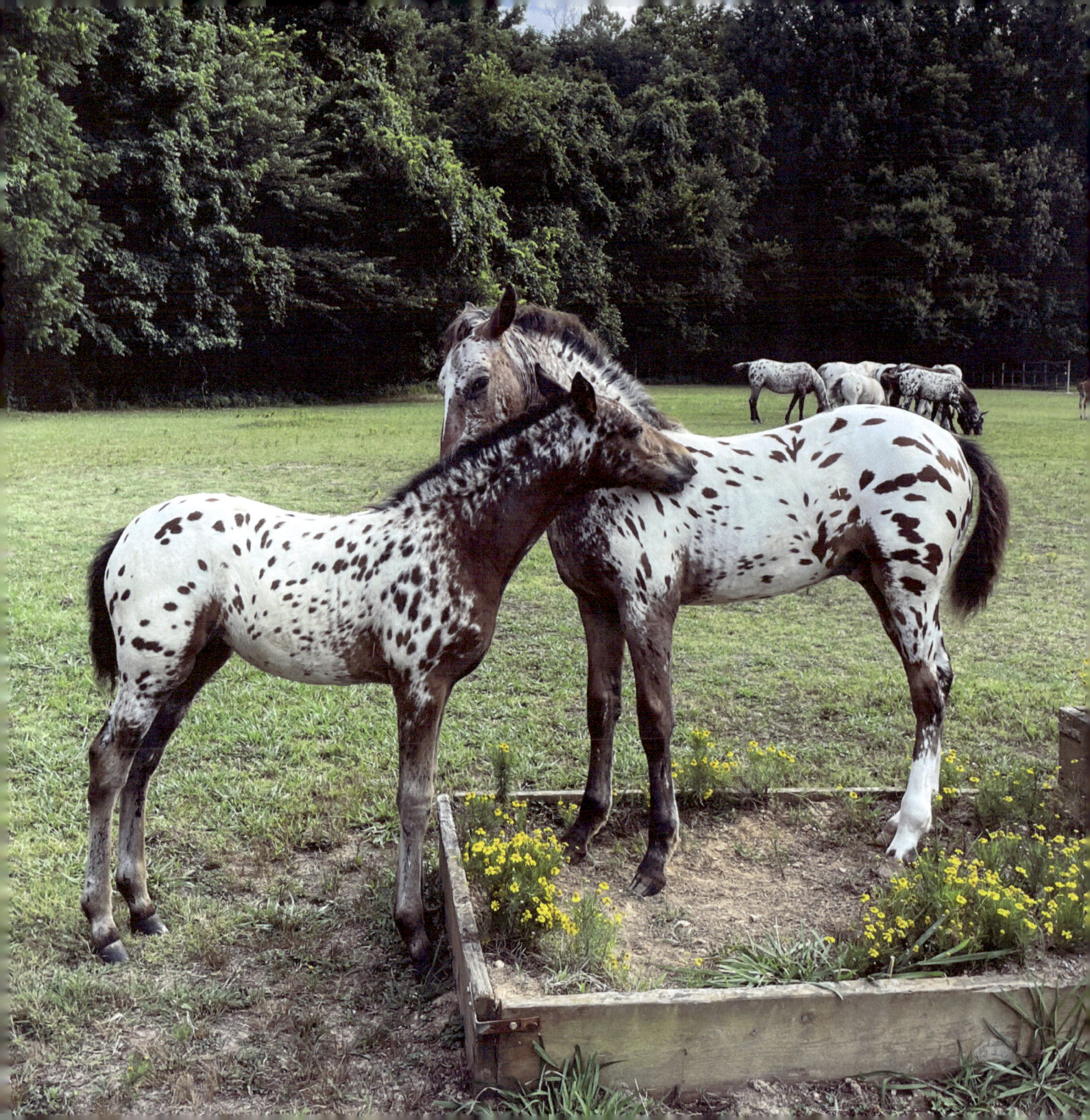

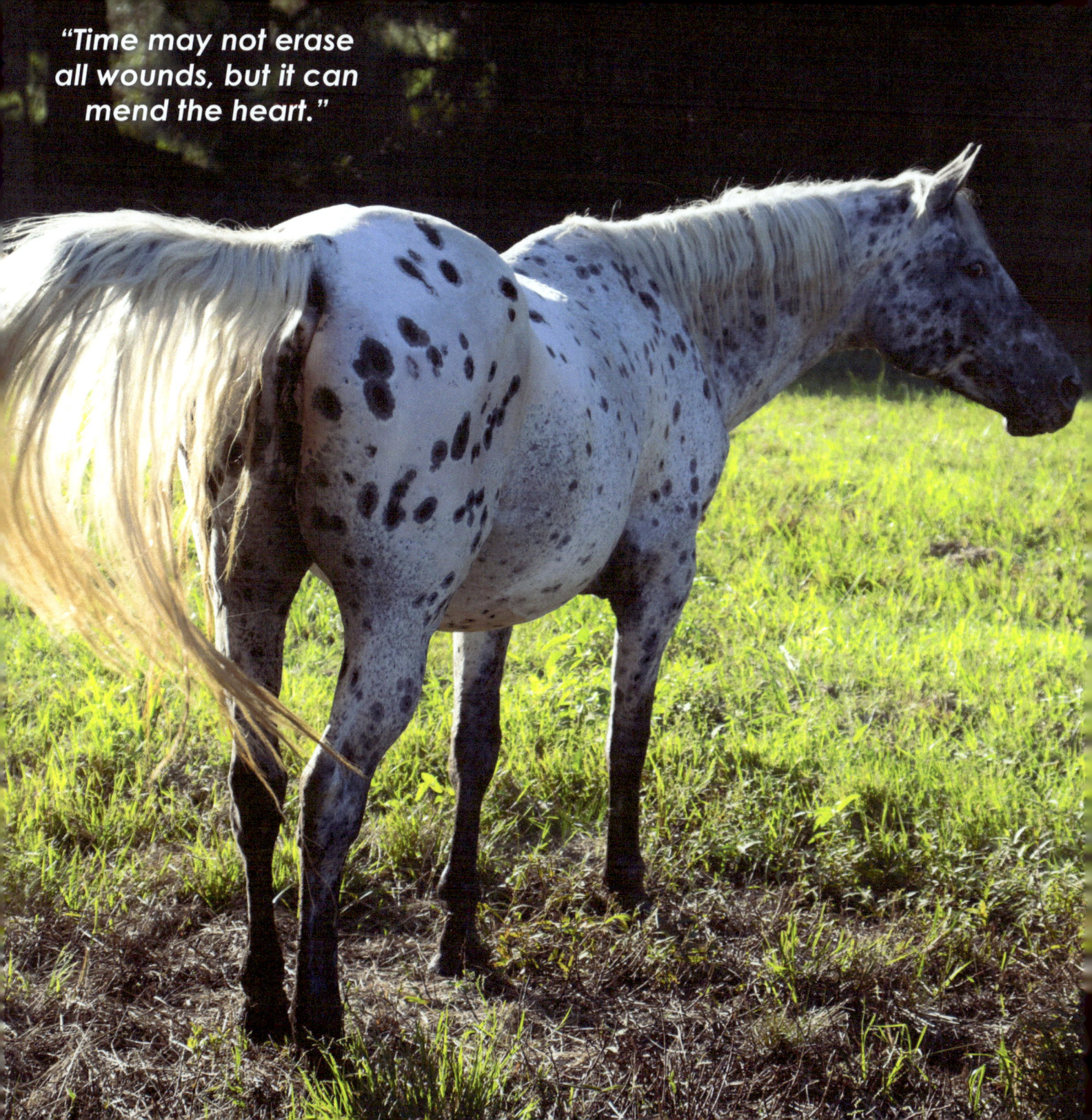

"Time may not erase
all wounds, but it can
mend the heart."

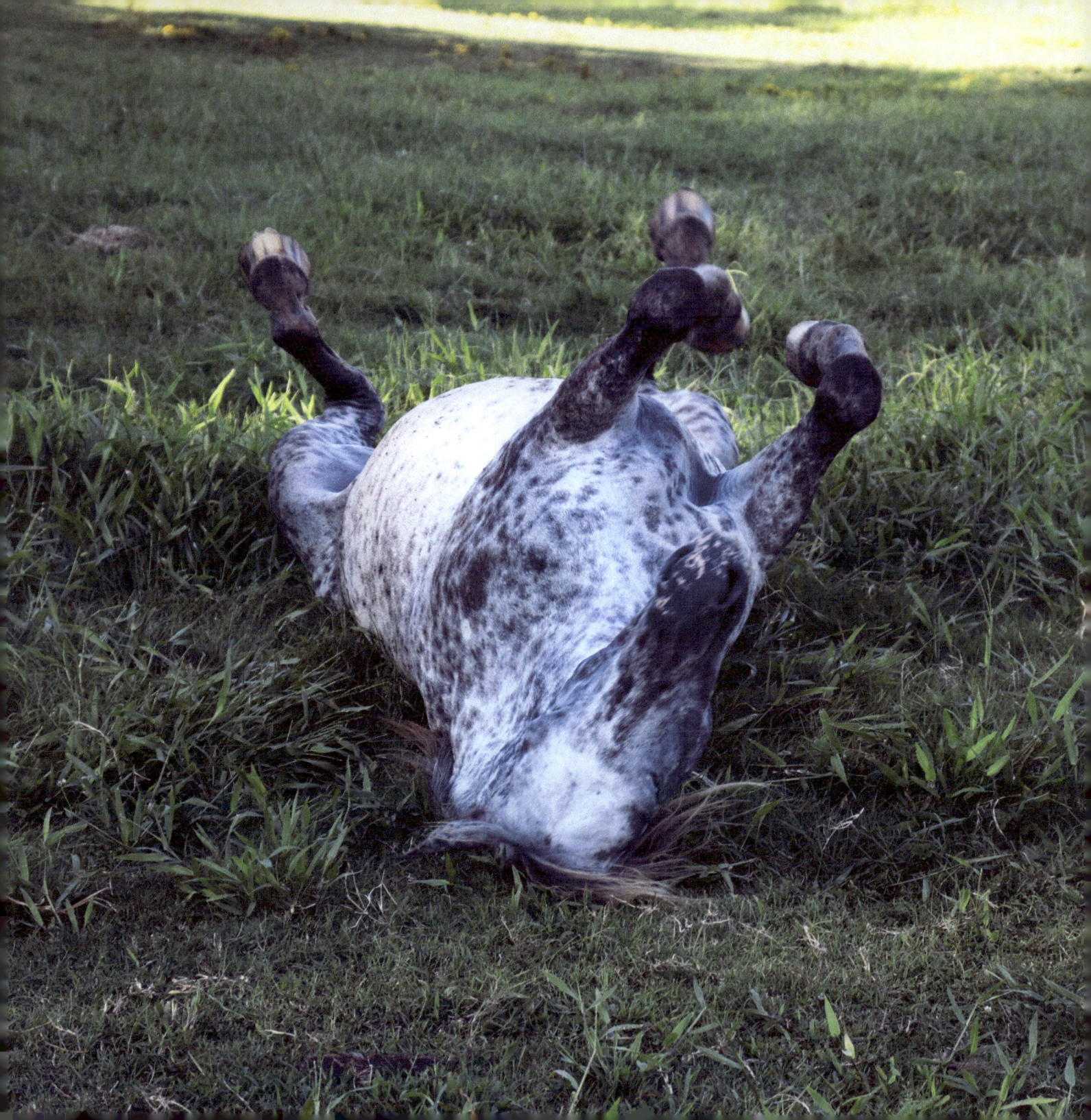

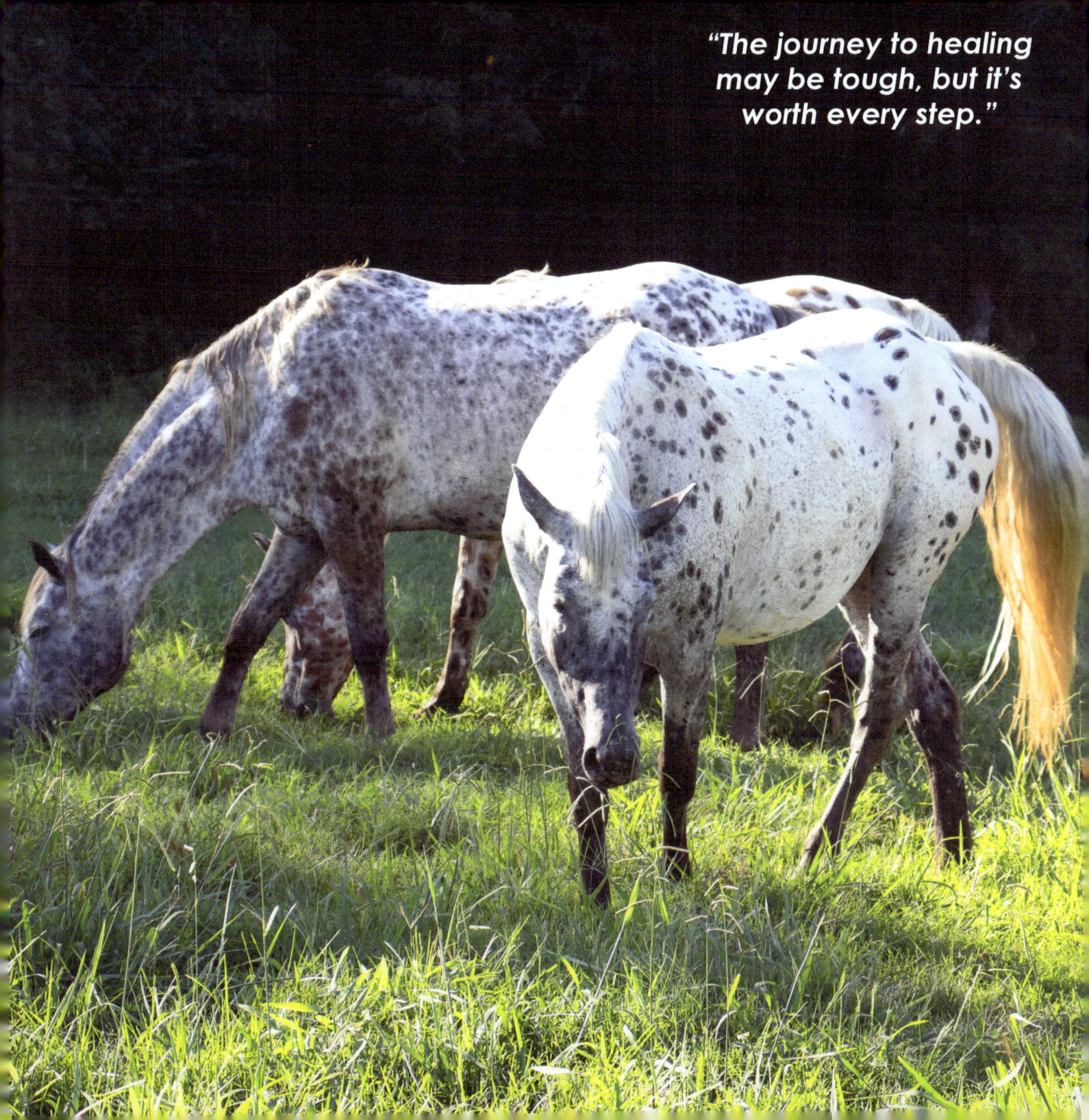

"The journey to healing may be tough, but it's worth every step."

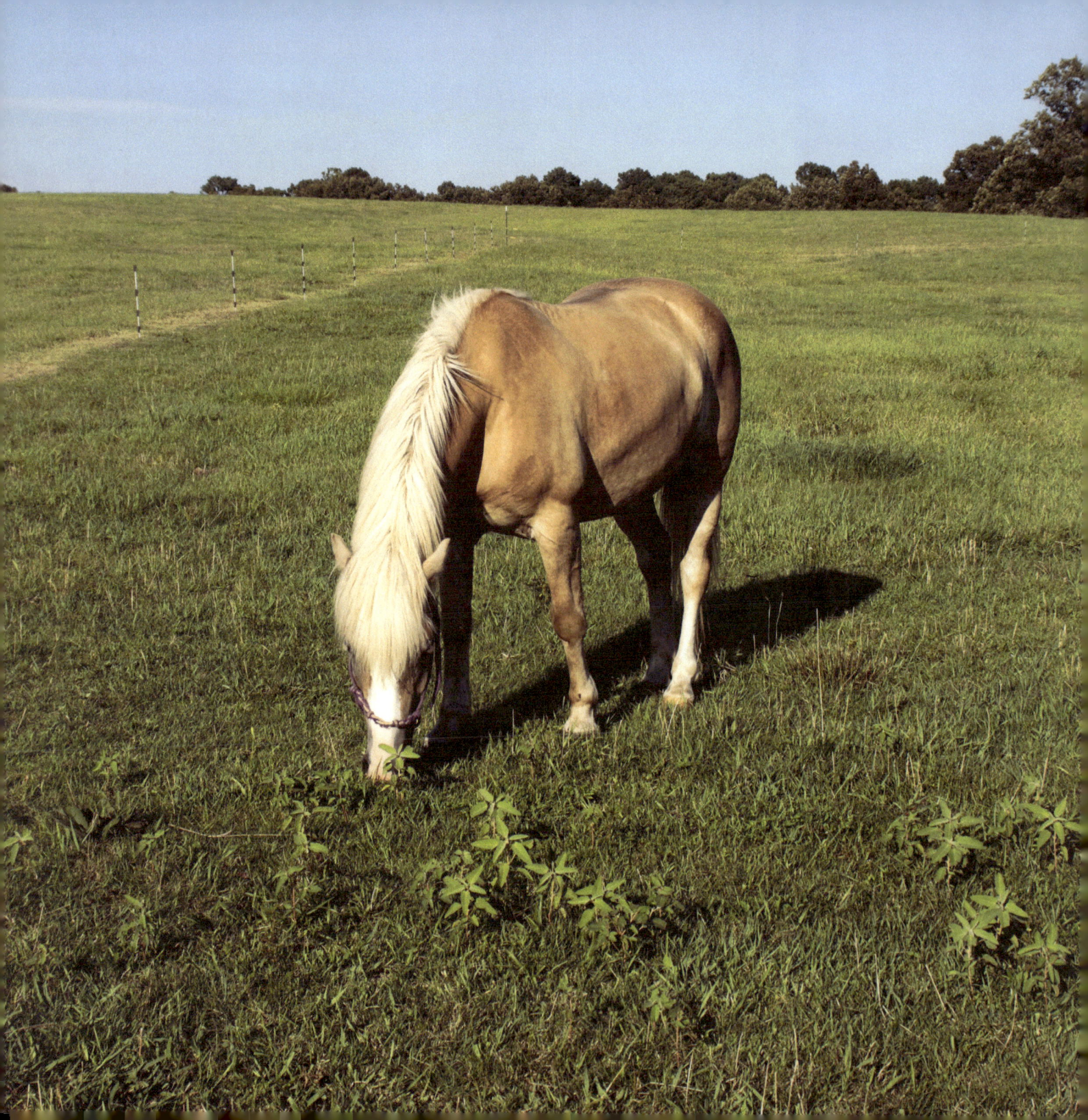

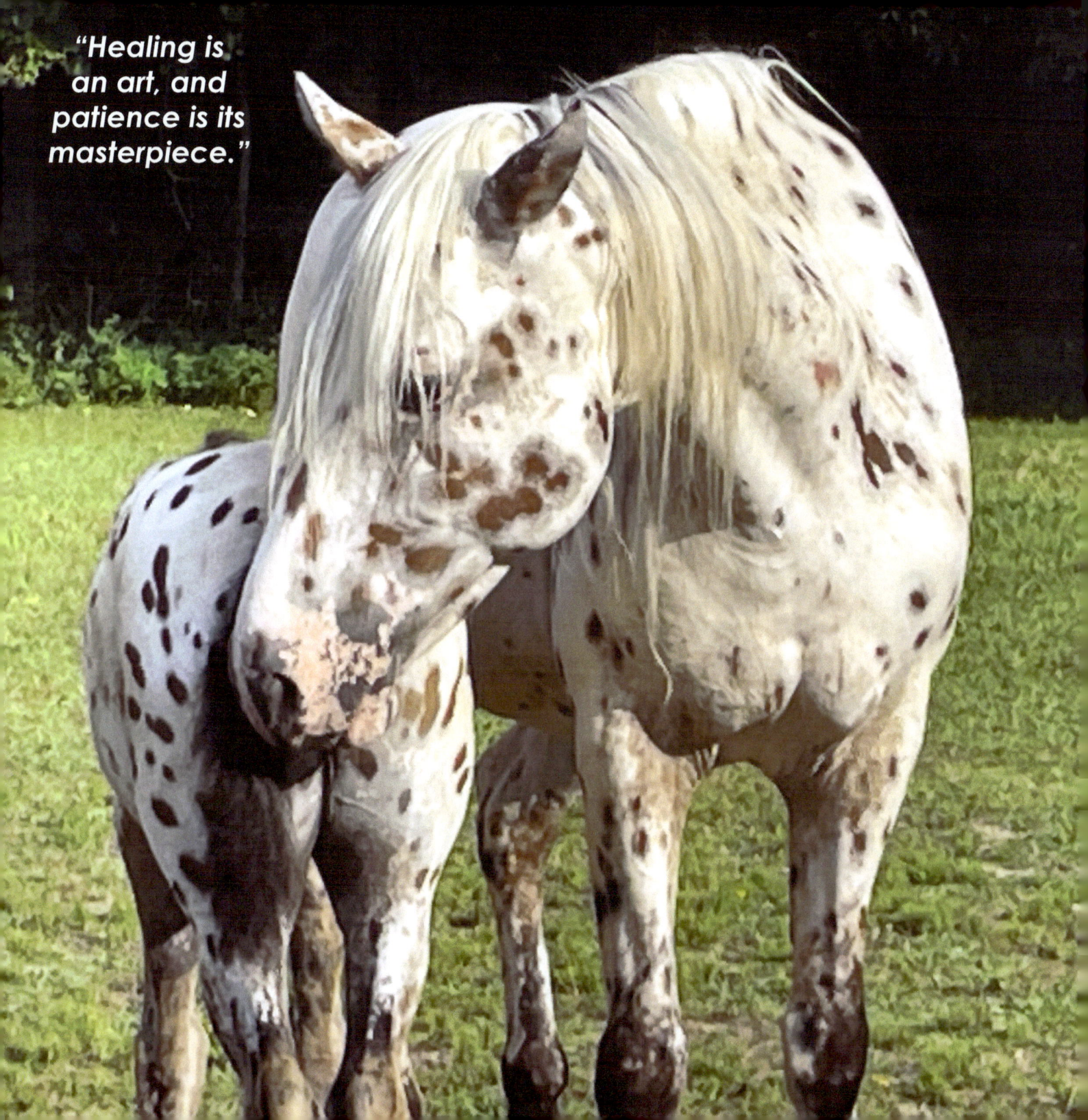

"Healing is an art, and patience is its masterpiece."

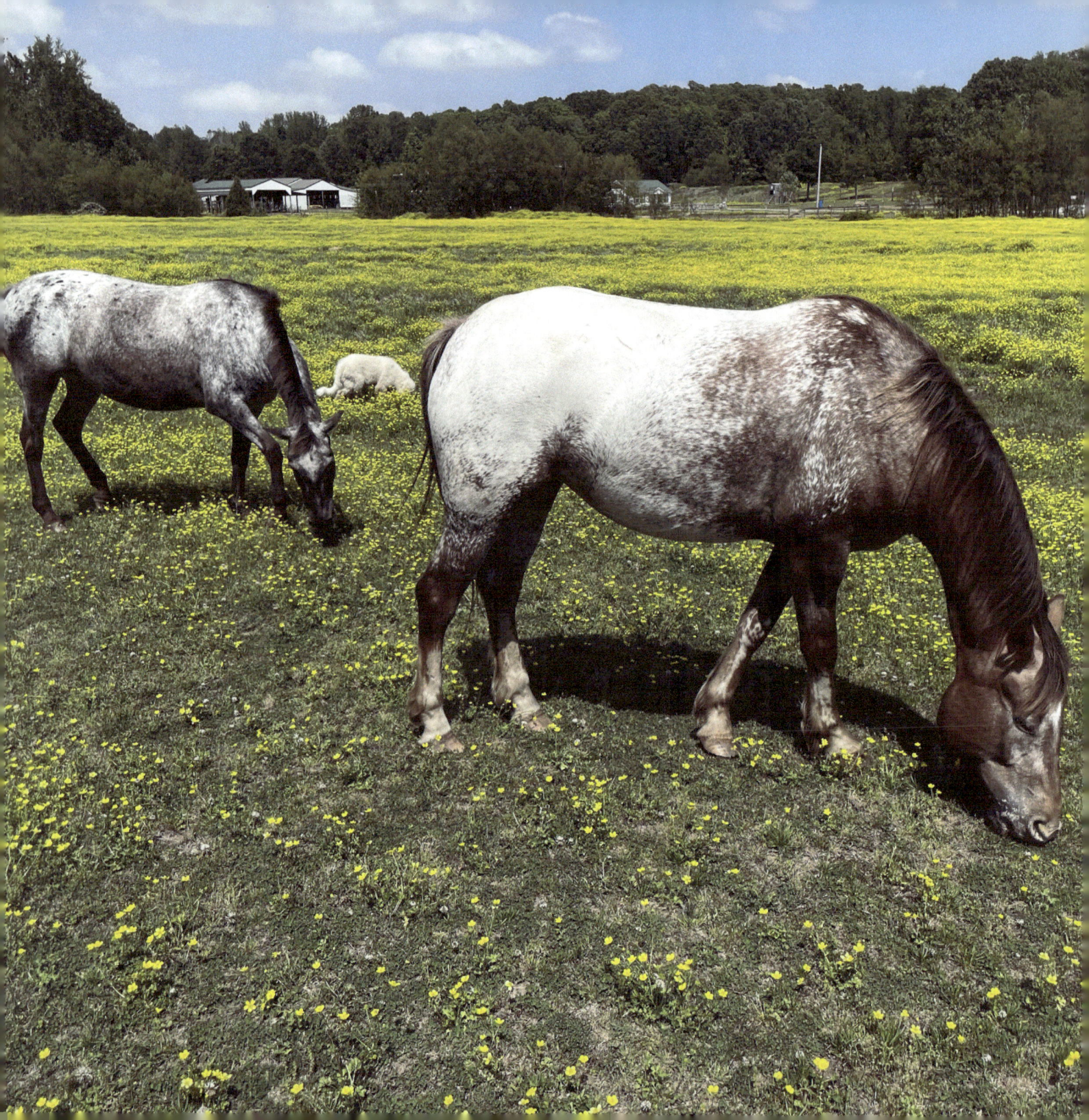

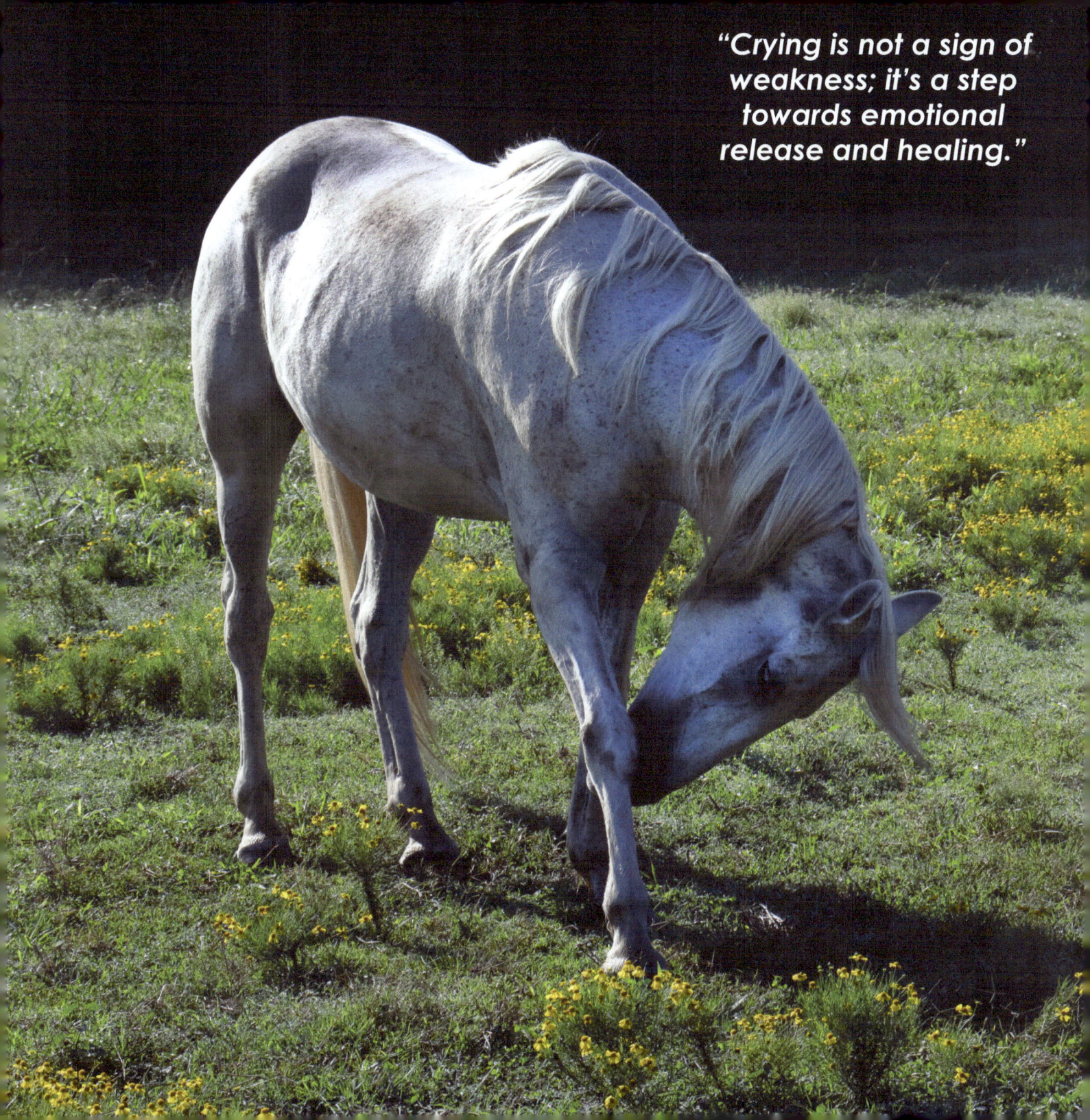

"Crying is not a sign of weakness; it's a step towards emotional release and healing."

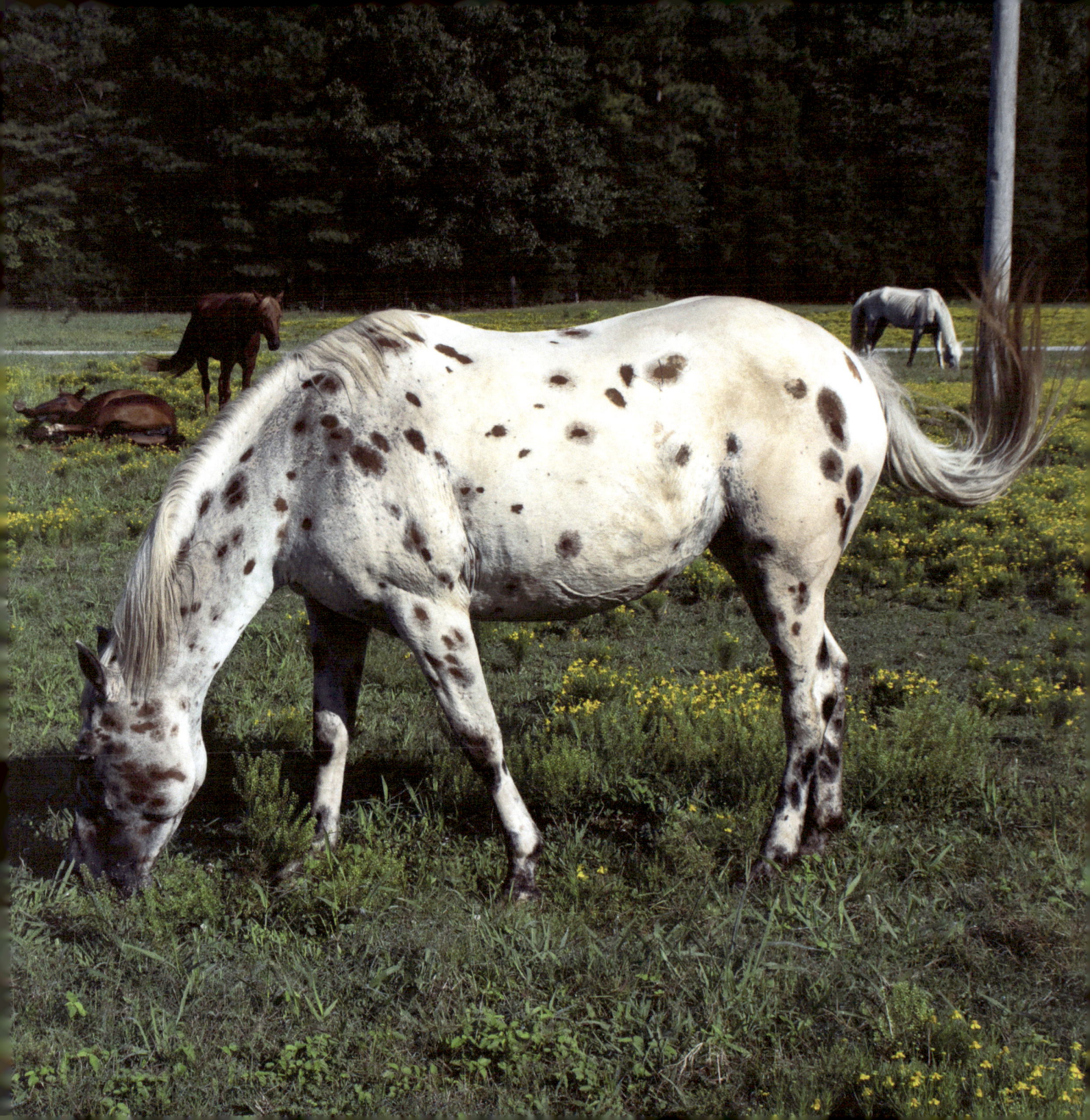

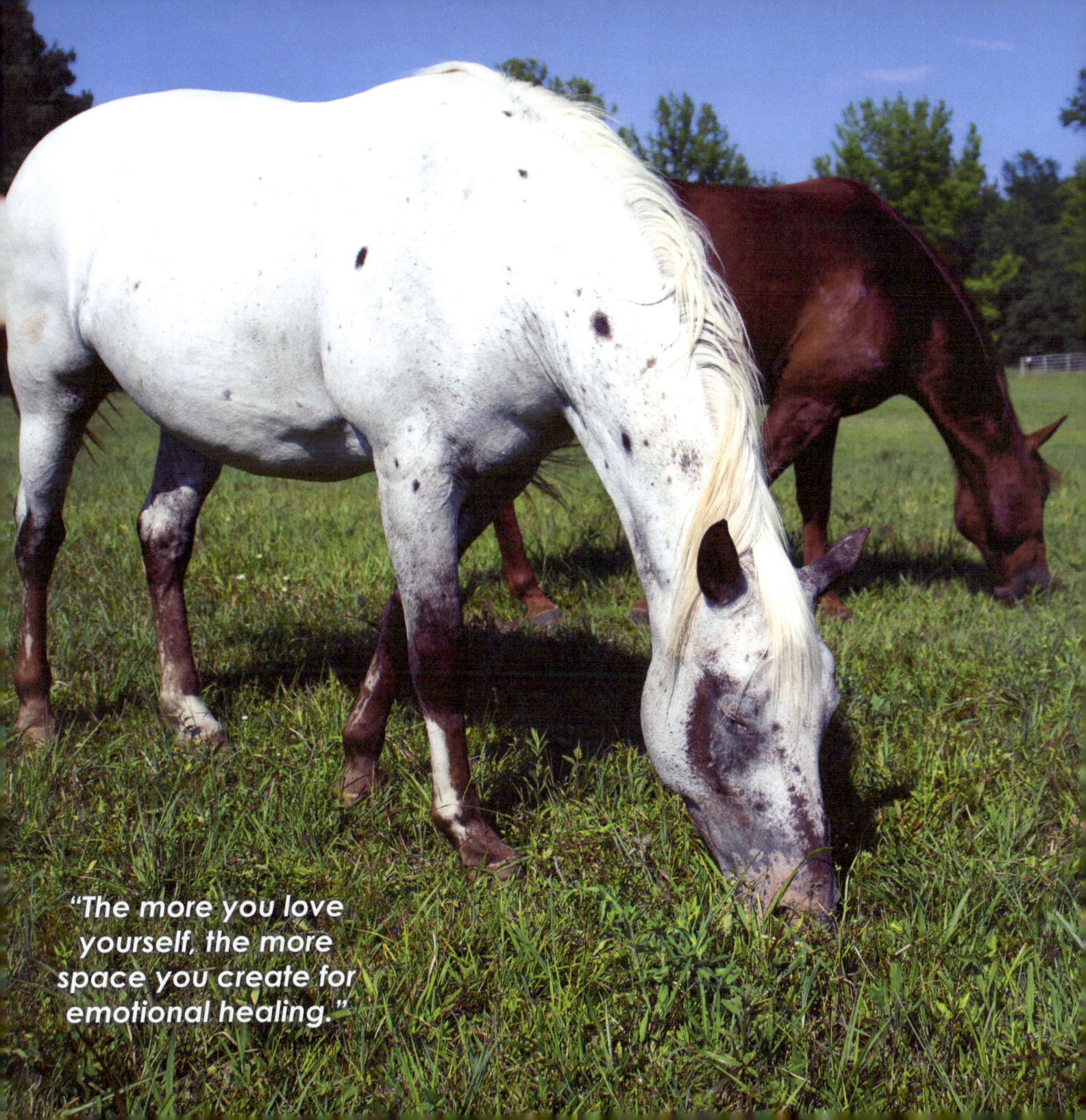

"The more you love yourself, the more space you create for emotional healing."

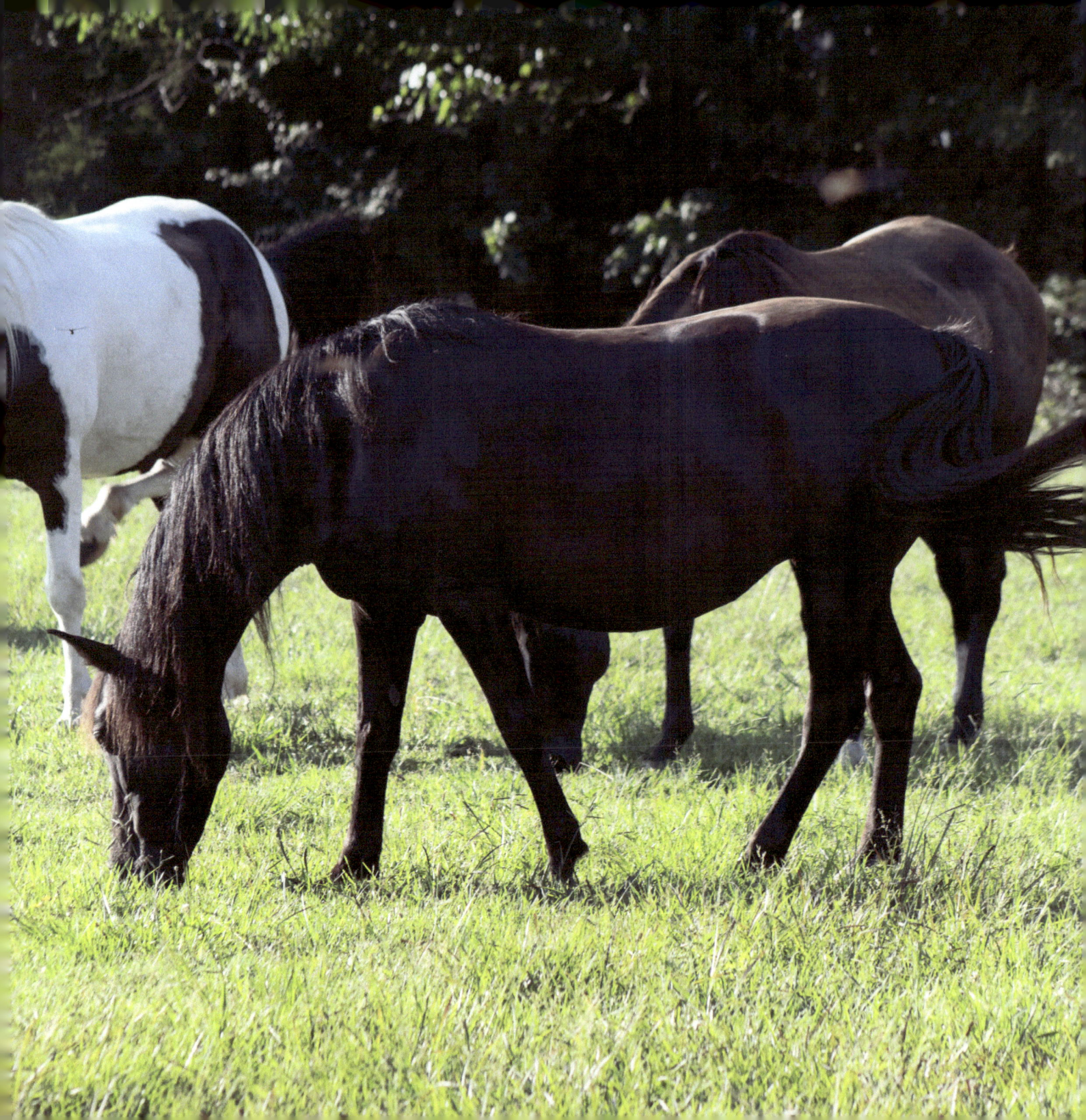

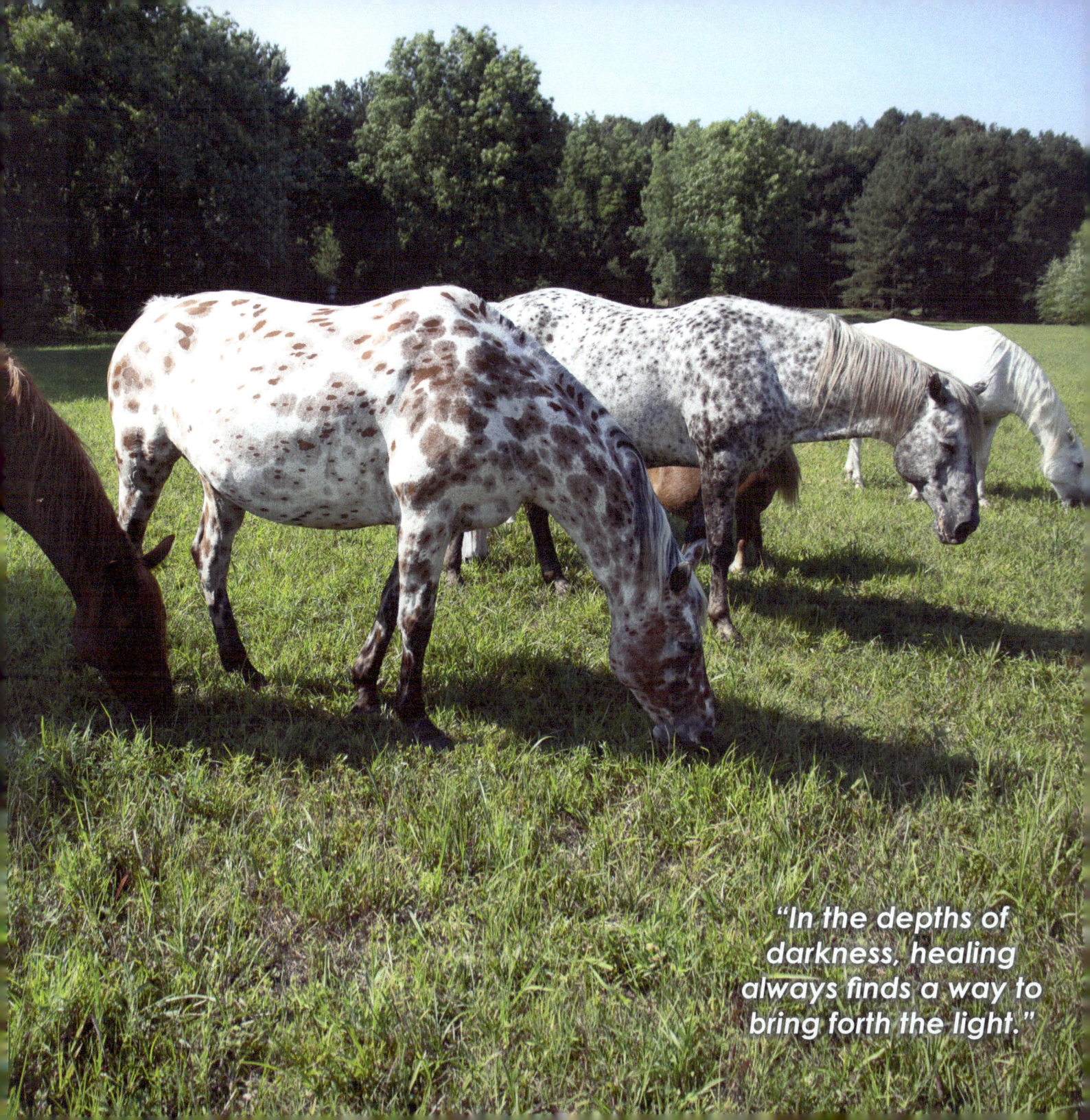

"In the depths of darkness, healing always finds a way to bring forth the light."

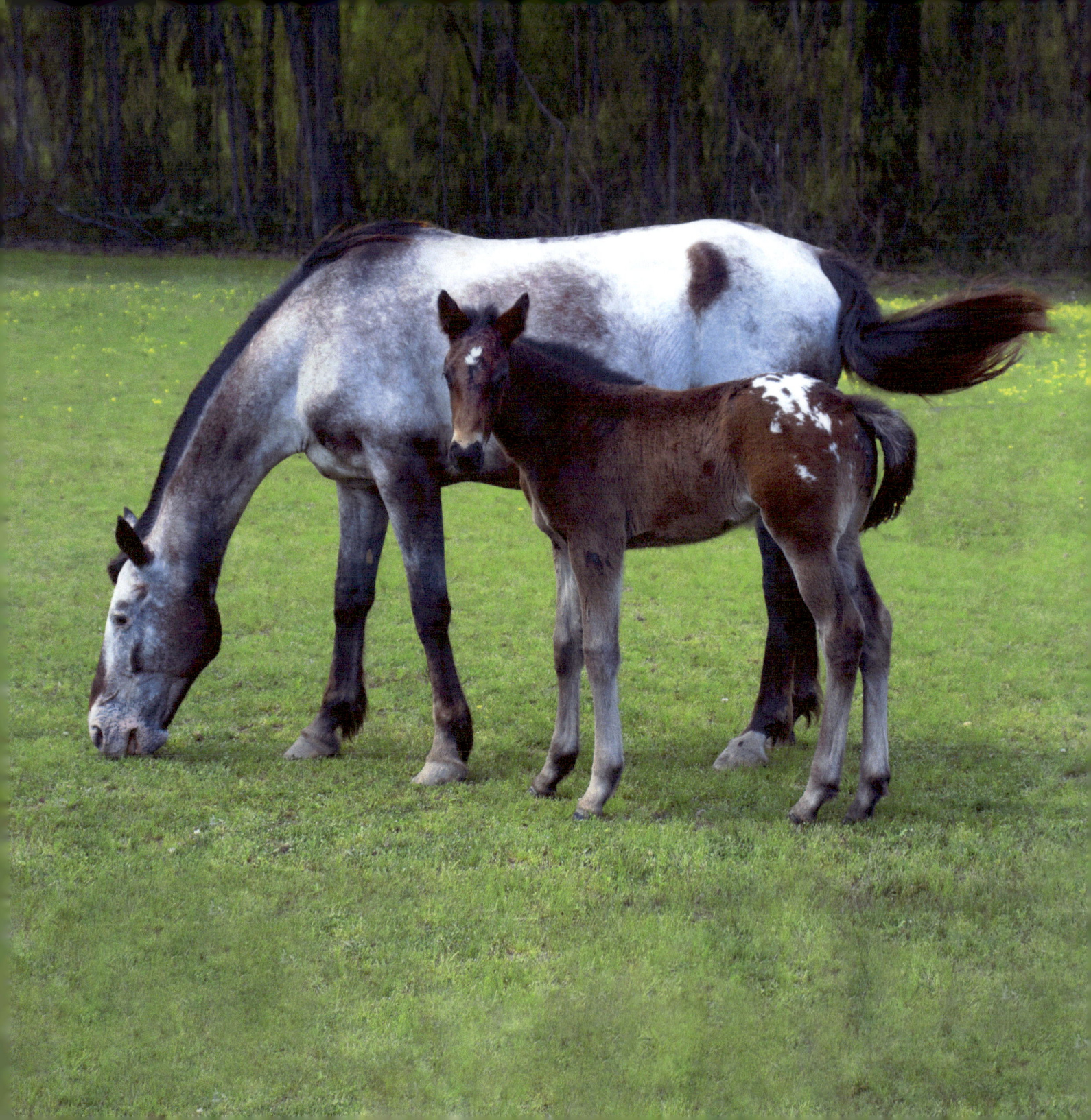

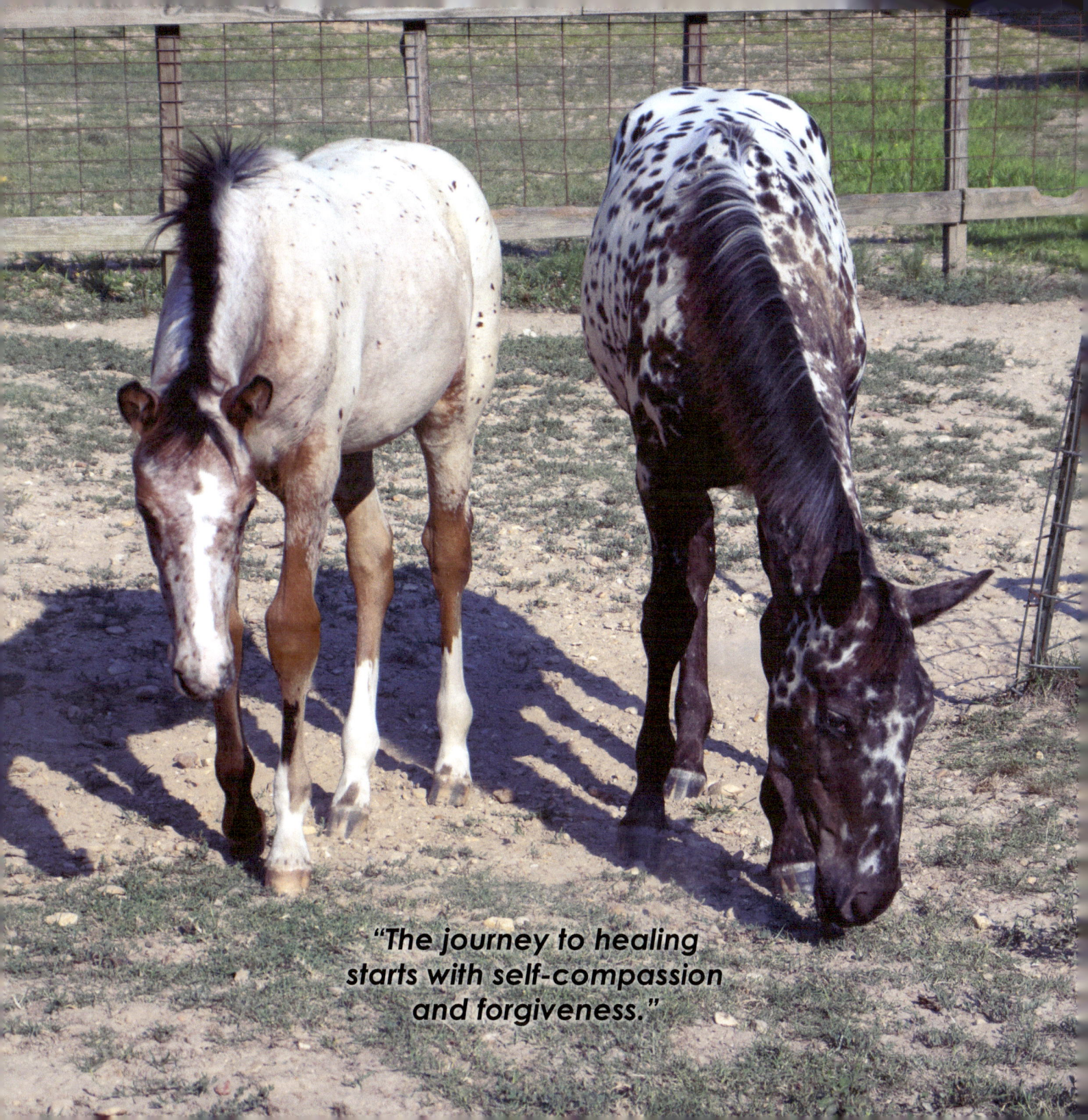

"The journey to healing
starts with self-compassion
and forgiveness."

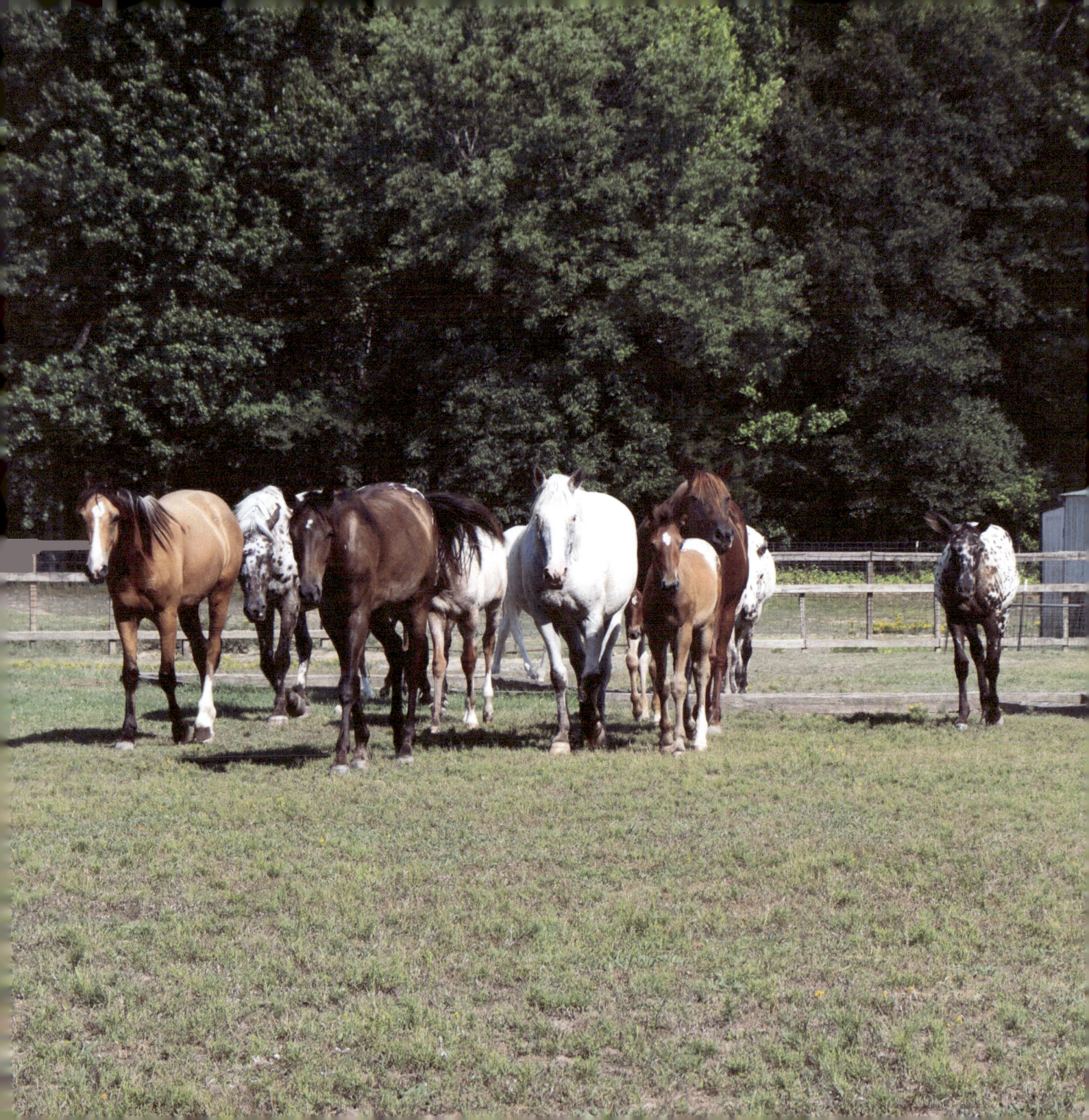

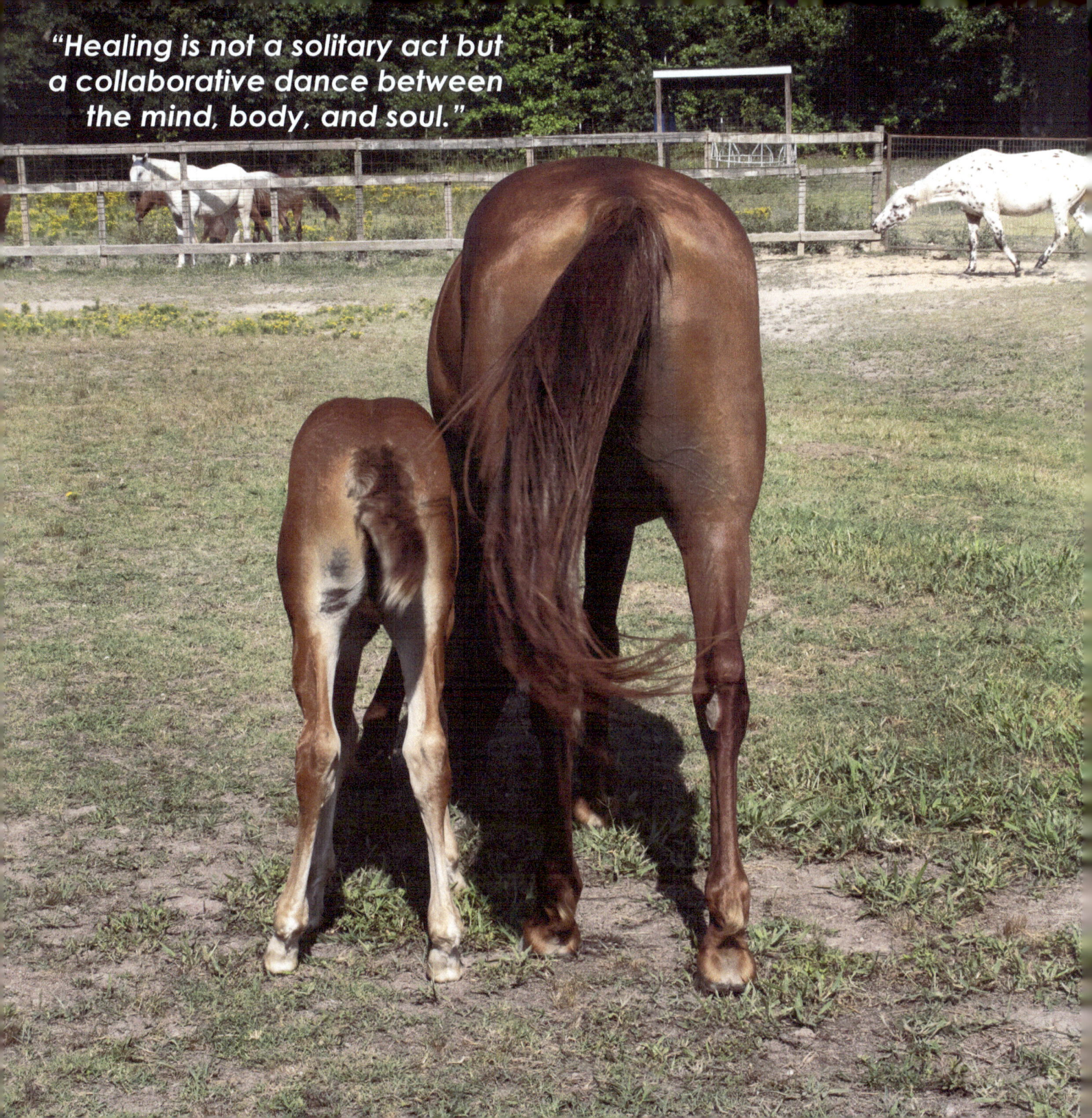

"Healing is not a solitary act but a collaborative dance between the mind, body, and soul."